FOOD, BULLSHIT, AND... OTHER COMPLICATIONS

ALEX FENOT

Legal stuff
(don't worry, it's not too long.)

Published by Foodnbullshit.
Printed in France/United States.
First edition: 2026
Legal deposit: 1st quarter 2026.
ISBN: 979-8-9931095-7-2 (Paperback Edition).

This book is a work of non-fiction.
The opinions expressed are strictly those of the author, which means you are not required to agree, applaud, chant, or feel comfortable.

Any resemblance to real people, restaurants, institutions, habits, trends, or situations—past or present—is either intentional, coincidental, or a reflection of how small the world actually is.

This book was written without filters, without algorithms, and without a kids' menu.

No fast-food chain was harmed during the writing of this book.
Even though some of them clearly deserved it.

Prologue

So here I am again, in front of you.
This is the second volume of my gastronomic outbursts.
I really thought I was done with all this.
Turns out I was dead wrong.

I wrote the first book in the dark. Teeth clenched, out of breath, like my ass was on the fucking grill. It was a punch in the mouth. It yanked me out of my lethargy and kept me from burning alive from the inside—hence the title.
I gave you an honest testimony about what happens in kitchens and dining rooms.
Of the job, what it was and what it is today.
What it does to us, mentally and physically—chewing you up and spitting you out.
About the people you can meet there, those who serve, cook, or dine.
And finally, an unfiltered look at a world moving at breakneck speed, changing... not always for the better, at least in my book.
Too often, leaving people on the side of the road.

Looking back, I now see that book for what it was: a confession, in a way.
Raw.
Messy.
Exhausted.
With a healthy dose of cynicism and sometimes without grace or elegance. I'll own that.

You might even say erratic; sure, why the hell not?
Mea culpa.
Not everyone gets to be Anthony Bourdain.
Was I too much in your face? Maybe.
Was it honest? Abso-fucking-lutely.
It came straight from the guts. It was rough and caustic, with a hint of spite in it as well.
As for the punches I threw—including the ones aimed right back at myself—were they justified? Deserved?
Ah... that's where it gets tricky.
Most of them? Yeah.
The rest was a stew seasoned with a dash of provocation and a touch of my natural stupidity.
The only organic ingredients in the book.
I won't lie; I took a sadistic pleasure in writing every goddamn line of it.
It was a breath of fresh air; it felt good.
Somehow, it was a cathartic experience.
So I will not apologize for any of it.
The only thing I can say for sure is the way I let it all fly was neither an accident nor a coincidence.
It went all over the place. It turned out exactly how I love my kitchen during a service:
A spiral that goes out of control and turns into an exquisite chaos.

Some questions remain, though.
What was I hoping to find, laying myself out, butt naked like that, without shame or restraint?
Have I found anything at the end of the road?
The answer is yes.

But to my surprise, it wasn't wisdom, and definitely not redemption—not a fucking chance for that.
What I got was exactly what I needed the most. Something simpler, more attainable, within reach.
Peace.
And honestly, that worked for me.
I even reread it a few days ago, with a weird kind of tenderness. And it made me laugh, because in all fairness, the book smells, reads, and breathes me.
So—mission accomplished.

Since then, I've calmed down. Well... most of the time.
But it didn't silence my doubts, my laughter, my rants, or my blow-ups. Those are still there.
I'm just less on edge.
Less busy fighting everything for sport and more willing to enjoy what's still standing in front of me.
I finally reached the state of mind where I can be honest about myself and true to the craft.
And a little more bearable for the others.
From now on, I promised myself that whatever life throws at me, I would "try" to deal with it with temperance.
With a dose of melancholy.
A little romance.
A hint of rebellion.
French romanticism, basically.

And this book—that's what it is, how it feels.
It's the after.
The calm after the storm, some comfort after the carnage.
But this one I did not write from the kitchen; I wrote it sitting down in the dining room at a restaurant table.
As a customer.
Yes, my dear Alice—let's take a look at the other side of the mirror.
A customer who eats at restaurants and has spent his entire life working in them. And with age, years, scars, and cuts, you can imagine I've seen plenty of hits and misses. Over time I've developed a memory, a palate, experience, and an opinion.
And inevitably... a preference.
And obviously... a dislike.
This is where it will sting a bit.
But, from now on, here, no battles and no more fights. No shouting and no raging fire licking the ceiling. Just a controlled flame.
But be careful...
Even on low heat, you can still get burned.
And you will; I'll make sure of that.
Believe me, I haven't gone soft, and I still have a corrosive tongue and a sharp eye. So, if I were you, I would not get too comfortable.
I will drop nasty lines along the way.
You know me; I can't help myself.
Venom is part of the flavor, and so is sarcasm.
And I fully intend to use both as seasoning.

So you can bet your ass that the menu is going to be spicy.
The starters will be salty.
The main courses will be served steaming hot.
And dessert?
Bittersweet.

Now let's be crystal clear:
This is not a recipe book, a food guide, or a culinary manual. I won't tell you what you should eat or how to cook it.
It's not the purpose of the book.
The idea was not to write a pamphlet or a manifesto against these modern times; I'm not here to lecture anybody, and I'm not preaching anything.
I don't have to.
Because whether you like it or not, our food says more about us than anything else, and cravings tell far more than appetite ever will.
Both define us.
I wrote this the way I cook—with appetite.
To bring back a memory, a moment etched into your mind.
Yeah, that one.
That dish you once ate—I'm sure you remember.
I know you recall those simple pleasures.
The ones we forget, neglect, and sometimes sacrifice on the altar of shoulda and woulda.
Not sure that applies to many things or people these days.
See, I am not biting anymore, and that's exactly what we are going to talk about.

Something intimate.
Like the feeling of a caress.

I'm inviting you on a journey, a short getaway into two worlds. Two ways of eating and two very different ways of living.
But we'll look at them not through politics.
Not through sociology or addictions, although we'd have plenty to talk about on both sides.
But through food and bullshit.
Because that's the one thing we all have in common.
I am taking you to a magical place where cooking and eating stop being a commodity and become a refuge again.
A temple ruled by discreet eroticism.
Yes, I said it.
The eroticism of food.
When butter becomes a lubricant for the soul, it flows like a memory.
It nourishes and feeds.
It heals, comforts, and repairs.
And when it's spread on a warm, crusty baguette cracking under your fingers, it feels like... happiness.
Tell me that's not tenderness.
That does more for me than a décolleté.
A slab of rillettes with gherkins turns me on more than lingerie.
And to enjoy it, all I have to do is take a bite of it.
Then rinse my lips with a glass of wine that softens my tongue and stains the tablecloth.

So, are you ready to commune in joy, tumult, grease, and grace?
What if we made the return of sin a way of life?
Let this be the ultimate sacrilege.
The one that isn't meant to be "liked."
We don't preach moderation here.
We eat with passion.
We drag bread through the sauce.
We scrape the plate.
Without restraint or shame.
Without hiding.
We praise the vice of the senses and the beauty of excess.
Lust, gluttony, and voluptuousness.
What if we started with that?

Come, my dearly beloved, and step into this den of gastronomic debauchery. And behold the magnificence of culinary exuberance.
Get ready to sin on the right side.

Amen to that.

A few words
More than a few, actually.

What the fuck was I thinking?
What went through my twisted, sick mind when I started this journey?
Me, writing a book.
What the hell was I expecting?
Who the hell did I think I was?
Some wannabe John McClane-type antihero writer with a dangling cigarette and the killer lines at the end.
Anthony Bourdain?
Hunter Thompson?
Damn fool.

I was told, though, that writing was freedom.
Well, it was somehow—but not only that.
For me, it was more of a relief.
Understand that writing isn't an escape; it's quite the opposite. It's a struggle. A ruthless bare-knuckle fight with yourself.
You lay it all out, and you spill your guts.
It's emotional archaeology.
You dig through emotions no one asked to see.
You excavate shit that was buried for a reason.
You flash parts of yourself that weren't meant for daylight.
But what I was not aware of is what happens after your words are finally out there.
What follows once it's all printed, published, and thrown into the wild?

I'll tell you. I was left with a void that hit me like a sledgehammer. Knocked out by a feeling of loneliness and a silence that vibrated in the walls. It hummed inside my brain and stared right at me, with eyes locked into mine.
I felt exposed, vulnerable, and stripped of boundaries.
Out of breath.
For a while I just sat there, staring at the ceiling, at my laptop. Wondering what to do, thinking: "Now what?"
When something shifted.
Vanity crept in; ego started whispering.
My mood followed the sales; if they went up, slowed down, or just stalled.
At one point, most of the footsteps that grabbed my attention didn't belong to the ones I knew.
But to strangers.
I tried to catch the noise of a review or rating.
Comments and random messages showed up in fragments in two different languages.
I wrote the damn thing in English too. But both books have a different vibe, a different rhythm.
Same bones... but different blood.
So, I've pretty much had a bit of everything.
"Thank you."
"I laughed."
"I saw myself in this."
"You're an asshole."
"It sucks."
"Vulgar."
"Awesome."
"Unfortunately, true."

I want to reassure you, this feeling didn't last very long. I came back down fast because I knew why I wrote it.
And mostly the only thing that mattered to me was not how many people bought the book—it's that it got read, even if it's just by ten people.
Some liked it.
Some did not.
That's life.

Every time I meet someone, I am asked the same question:
"What does it feel like to write a book and be published?"
Honestly?
When it went live online, I was in front of my Mac. I felt some satisfaction, but nothing soul-shattering.
Holding the paperback, however, was a very different story.
I had it in front of me.
I felt the weight of its presence.
Watching my face on the cover.
Reading my name on the spine, my own goddamn words, engraved in ink forever, was a strange, almost unreal sensation. And that silent shock resonated so loudly, it rattled my cage.
I couldn't help feeling an overwhelming pride for the accomplishment.
I know it might not seem like much to some who consider it unworthy or trash.
But it's my trash, mine.

So I'll own it and wear it as fucking loud and proud as I can.

And yet, I somehow feel stuck between a rock and a hard place, ecstatic and skeptical at the same time.
Ecstatic because the book exists now.
Those pages I have worked on, laughed about, and bled for will reach people I'll never meet.
This story is alive;
It breathes and lives without me.
It circulates on screens, inside phones, on tablets, and in earbuds.
It gets downloaded and scrolled.
It sneaks in, then adapts between subway stops and push notifications.
I find it ironic, though, that the words I wrote are inside the same glowing rectangle that hypnotizes and hijacks everyone's attention.
My lines lie there; they coexist and share space with reels, the dopamine, and whatever algorithm is trending this week.
All those words on pages I gave were returned to me compressed in pixels in 4K.
The same message, but with a different filter.
It took me a moment to unzip the concept.

As for being skeptical,
All this we call progress feels to me like an erosion of silence and stillness in this hands-free existence that runs on an endless loop.

I just hope that this story, now stored in the digital warehouse, won't dissolve into feeds or into the static of everyday distraction.

Personally, I prefer paperback books.
It takes up space on a table or on a shelf.
It has weight in your hands and in your memory.
It doesn't circulate; it settles.
When you choose it, you can smell it, and you can feel it under your fingertips.
Sometimes you even pass it on and share the pleasure.
And you don't read the same way on a screen because it can exist everywhere at once.
A book requires a frame.
It sets its own rhythm and resists fragmentation.
It does not have the same sensuality; clicking and turning a page are not the same thrill.
On a screen, you consume, inform yourself, and gather information.
On paper, you absorb the words.
They go through you; they infuse.
They carry you somewhere.
But I fear that with time, those books would become relics.

That's the conflict of generations—not paper versus digital;
But object versus medium.
Meaning versus momentum.
Can you measure the depth of a text on a flat screen?

Does the speed of 5G let you see what's hiding behind a sentence?
What I regret isn't modernity; it's the loss of attention, the scattering.
This obsession with mobility and the compulsion of accessibility have become the words of the century. We live nowadays for what's immediate and what's quickly and easily comprehensible.
Then move on to what comes next.
We used to look for meaning; now we crave stimulation.
We even surrender to laziness, but not the kind that comes from tired bodies, but from the impatient minds that confuse scrolling with reading and liking with thinking.
Because the noise of the world just got too loud,
And we've been trained to move so fast that we forgot what slowing down means and what it feels like.
As for me, I became a guy who is still chasing meaning while everyone else is busy chasing algorithms.
Sometimes I wonder if I should've chopped all this into threads instead. Using fifteen-second videos, a calibrated smile, and that fake awful fry voice.
You know the kind.
The one that makes some sound wiser than they are and gives the illusion of saying something profound while barely touching the surface.
That's what the world wants nowadays, right?
Not words but content with a frivolous attitude.
Would I have sold more?

Well, I'll never know, because it's not me.
To be blunt, being consensual bores the fuck out of me. So I'll let influencers of appearances dance in their reel frenzy, and I'll stick with books.
And I'll sell what I sell.
Time will do the rest—or it won't.
I don't care.
It's okay; I wasn't planning on being author of the year, the critics' darling, or selling thousands.
Because this story is raw, imperfect, flawed, dented, and somehow still a work in progress.
In a nutshell, my life.

I am not worn out or jaded; I still smile at the thought that somewhere out there, a few strangers still sit down and read the old way.
When nobody's watching and in silence.
Away from the clamor. Broadening an imagination, enriching their vocabulary,
Isn't it what shapes a mind and builds a personality?
For that alone, I am grateful.
To write or publish is to wager that curiosity hasn't yet vanished. It is an act of faith in slowness, in depth, and in the quiet weight of attention.
Reflection.
Because a book has layers, and you have to sit with it.
Digest it.
Sometimes wrestle with it.
It doesn't fit inside a comment, and it doesn't dance. It doesn't sell itself in ten seconds.

It’s not a vibe, a mood, or a clip.
It takes time, demands silence, and requires commitment.
Stillness.
Like love.

Some of my friends or some close to me have not read it. I don’t blame them—I assume they have their reasons.
Maybe they’re not ready because they know they won’t like what they find inside. Or maybe they know those pages concern them too. Because I didn’t write it for the crowd, I wrote it for my wife.
For my daughter.
And a little for myself.
Because every sentence is a breadcrumb leading back home, to what matters.
A way to be seen, to be understood beyond the noise I make and the space I take.
A way of saying, This is who I am, behind the mask.
The more I think about it, it turns out I didn’t write a book—I wrote my testament.
A last will in digital and paperback.
Some public last words.
I know they’ll read it one day.
When the house is quiet and my voice exists only in print.
When it’s safe to open those pages without having to face and look in the eyes of the man who wrote them.
That’s how it goes, I guess.

We put our lives in writing for the living and end up being understood when we're dead.

Nevertheless, I'll let the words go where they're wanted... out there, among the anonymous hands, eyes, and ears of those who still know how to sit still and listen.
I don't mind if you keep on scrolling; I'd rather be out of sync than be a thread.
I'll choose being irrelevant over being insignificant.
That's why books aren't relics of the past but echoes that travel through time, and they matter.
But to write one...is to accept becoming, yourself, a voice from another different time.
It's funny; I'm in the cloud now. And yet still very much alive down here.
If my words keep echoing in this digital world long after I'm gone—damn, I can live with that.
Fine by me.
But know that it wasn't planned;
It was by accident.
It wasn't strategic;
It was an unexpected collision of circumstances.
That's as good as it gets, right?
And maybe that's enough.
But is it good enough for me not to write another one?
No.
Sorry.
Forget what I said; I'm not sorry.
Because...
The pleasure is all mine.

So, let's start then.

Special of the day

I am French.
I'm fifty-three.
I am an executive chef.
People who read my first book already know that.
I'm saying it for the others.
And as we're going to talk about food or meals, don't take me for a fool, and it's better not to feed me bullshit or word salads. Unless you add pancetta or guanciale, a poached egg, and garlic croutons. Or even better—gizzards, chicken livers. There you go—now we're talking; we have a proper "Landaise" salad.
All of this to say: I've got a bit of experience in the matter.
Hell, by page twenty-seven I'm already hungry.
Not a great start.

I won't beat around the bush.
Let's dive right into it and call it like it is.
I don't like this era.
It bores the fuck out of me.
No—I will rephrase.
It pisses me off.
That's about the only good thing: it doesn't leave me indifferent.
Because I can't stomach lukewarm and everything that is being watered down, polished, filtered, and softened.
It irritates me, to say the least.

I have the impression of living in an era where everything is mushy. Where I see and meet people who wrapped themselves in endless excuses not to take a stance or to keep their asses stuck between a rock and a hard place.
"I don't think anything."
"I don't have an opinion."
That kind of crap makes my skin crawl.

In general, I don't like trends, so don't ask me to follow any. So you won't be surprised to learn that I'm not a fan of so-called trendy restaurants.
Especially the over-themed, concept-driven kind with their "Healthy & Free-From" menus.
Basically, meaning no butter, no fat, and no salt.
Let's not forget with sauce on the side and optional joy.
Plates designed for Instagram. Where everything is straight, clean, neat, and bland—just like this world that apologizes for existing.
Sad appetizers for clients who eat like they're taking medicine. Thinking it'll make them immortal.
With main courses, you chew halfway with clenched teeth, finishing your meal with an empty stomach and a clean conscience.
Like a quinoa-and-tofu penitent.
And desserts with no sugar and no gluten.
In short: a cuisine without pleasure, without balls, without madness.
If that's your thing, no problem. Whatever works for you.
But it isn't mine.

Not my jam.
I love meals that sing, cooked by and for people who are still hungry.
Hungry for butter, flesh, authenticity, and honesty.
Hungry for the things we're no longer supposed to say, do, be, or taste—let alone laugh at jokes that aren't politically correct.
And since I've got you here, let me tell you this:
You exhaust me with your detox apps, your bullshit miracle diets, and your calorie counting.
As for the commandments:
"You shouldn't eat this."
"You should eat that."
I just can't take it anymore.
So, I'll stay civilized and simply say that politeness prevents me from telling you exactly what I do with that advice.
But I'm sure you get an idea.

Now that I've made my point, let's start this book already; enough foreplay.
It's time to get to the bottom of it.
I'm taking you on a trip to France.
A land where taste takes revenge on blandness, joy on fear, and red wine on smoothies.
Where recipes and food still mean something.
But I am talking about the kind you cook, not the one you throw in a microwave.
The kind you keep an eye on through the oven's glass.

The one you order—and savor—in brasseries, neighborhood bistros, corner joints, and dives that stay afloat by sheer miracle.
And fine dining too.
Yes—the whole nine yards
That's what makes this country rich: there's room for everybody and everyone's taste.
Restaurants that are the DNA of this country
Diverse and plural.
Messy.
Colorful.
Places that clash and oppose each other—yet those dining rooms still remind us of what fraternity means. They are loud and full tables with faces, voices, and excess.
Where servers bring plates with meaning and purpose for thrill-seekers and flavor junkies.
Meals with aromas perfuming the room with the scent of garlic, onion, wine, and beef stock.
Whispering in your ear the most beautiful music there is. An ode to orgies that sound like life, fat, and eternity.
All cooked, served, and eaten by larger-than-life characters—with their moods, their overflows, and their emptiness.
And sometimes... their bullshit too.
Yep, that too.

So let's rise, my possessed-by-taste friends, heretics of pleasure, whose joy is sitting at a restaurant table.

And you, the ones behind a stove or in the dining room, waiting to get crushed without mercy in this enchanted inferno.
I invite you to discover a sociology drowning in Burgundy sauce.
Psychology glazed with veal jus.
Philosophy drowned in béchamel.
A religion whose commandments don't teach you the difference between good and evil,
but right from bland.
That's the way I see the world.
That's the way I live in it.
Wait, I'm not building a church or a cult here; I could not if I wanted to; I can't change a fucking light bulb. But I turned this existentialism into a crusade.
Yeah.
But not against people.
Against self-righteousness and moral posturing.
Against blandness served on a sad plate.
Against everything that replaced flavor with guilt.
I'm neither Rabelais nor Falstaff, and I don't want to convince anybody otherwise.
I'm not looking for disciples or followers.
I'm looking for guests.

I know this book won't please everyone.
Because we are going to talk about taste. As it is subjective, it won't be to the liking of militant vegans or happiness accountants. Cellophane-wrapped wellness gurus. Plain yogurt crusaders or lukewarm tempeh apostles.

Because here, the only dogma is the pleasure of eating.
So, whether you read this while opening a bottle of wine, or dancing in your kitchen, or even sitting on the John.
Think of this as a prayer for well-being.
A hymn to edible flesh.
A love letter to the food that rattles the brain and shakes the soul.
Let's celebrate menus like poems, bread like an embrace, and wine like a confession. And screw the skinny silhouettes counting their steps.
Speaking of which—we won't be counting anything here.
Not calories.
Not indigestion.
Not liver attacks.
And definitely not culinary orgasms.
We won't give a rat's ass about photoshopped plates or diets.
Too bad for the shamans; no seeds on the menu today.
Let's stuff our faces and mop up the sauce. Lick the bottom of the plate and laugh with our mouths full and raise our glasses.
There will be fat.
Happiness.
And wine that warms the soul and fucks up your liver.
A joyful mess that shapes an ideal better than any half-baked doctrine.
A shitstorm of debauchery that builds a country better than any political speech.

And for those whom I lost somewhere between
Falstaff and Rabelais
You're going to have to make an effort and keep
up.
Pay attention, damn it.
Don't start me up, or shit will hit the fan.

Welcome to France.

From Paris, with spite

Welcome to Paris.
Well, you know what I mean.
Because if there's one thing the French are not... it's welcoming.
When you're fresh off the plane, it kind of slaps you in the face. After a couple of days, you settle in and get used to it.
But if you ever get lost in the city or need help, a Parisian will always offer you one of two very distinct answers.

First option:
"Don't know."
The guy was born here. He lives here. But the second you ask him something, he suddenly develops full-blown amnesia.
You could ask him for directions, his address, or his own name, and you'd get the same reply.
"Don't know."
Dickhead.
Think about your next trip; you might end up in the middle of Times Square. What happens if you need to go to the Meatpacking District?
Let's see how that feels.

Then you have the second one.
Nice. Polite. Friendly.
He wants to help you so badly that after giving you directions, he or she might walk you to your destination.

And honestly, it's probably the safest option, because let's be blunt:
Have you ever heard a French person speak English?
Not one who lives abroad, but one in his natural habitat.
It's hilarious, unintelligible gibberish. A mix of French, Spanish, and English. A soup of onomatopoeia and invented words that would make any linguist lose their mind.
So yes, he will help you, but I'm not sure he helped himself.

Now, if you're lucky, you might have asked a French person for a few tips before your plane touched down.
I, whether in the restaurant or at social gatherings, am constantly cornered by people who've just planned a week in France.
They want the 'must-eat' list.
They want the 'to-do' list.
As I've lost count of how many Americans have returned home horrified, telling me we are 'particular' people. I've even printed little cards that I keep in my wallet to hand out freely.
My own version of a diplomatic warning.
And my tip is always the same. Friendly, but blunt.
You've got it all wrong.
The most important thing isn't what to do;
It's what not to do.

Because there is one thing we have absolutely no sense of humor about: it's gastronomy.
It is the last territory we have left where we can truly open our mouths. When it comes to the table, we become touchy, irritable, and borderline rigid. Some might call us 'pains in the ass.'
You can say it. I'll agree.
So, to maximize your experience in my country, here is my advice:
Once the sightseeing is done and you are starving, you will find a 'cute' little restaurant. But before you push that door and take a seat...
We need to talk about the rules of engagement.
I have classified these "faux pas" by severity—from 'acceptable' to a 'straight red flag.'
Pay attention to the last five.
They are non-negotiable.
If you break them, the consequences can be catastrophic.
So don't screw up.

Here's the list:

— Telling the server you visited France twenty-four years ago in a city you can't pronounce correctly.
We don't care.

— Trying to speak French.
No. Don't.

—You want to eat family style, sharing plates.
We're not on Instagram.

—Smiling at the waiter.
What the hell is wrong with you?

—Refusing the wine list.
Rude. Want a Coke instead? Yeah, I thought so.

—Having dinner with a cocktail.
We're not in an airport lounge.

— Telling the server to ask the chef to split a meal in two plates
You go ask him; I am staying here and watching.

— Asking the server to split the check four ways.
Your problem. Do the math.

— Asking for ketchup.
Pardon?

— Ordering your meat above medium.
Troglodytes.

— "Could I get a doggy bag for the leftovers?"
Come on, Cowboy-the-fuck-up and finish your plate.

"Et voilà."
That being said, if you want to understand the French—or France—there's no need to visit museums. Just go to the supermarket or look at what's on our plates.
Because the only way to get us is through the gut.

And the timing is perfect;
We are about to step inside a restaurant.
I hope you’re hungry.
Me?
I’m starving.

Ex cathedra

I am not into religion; I don't have that kind of faith. Never did.
Not in God, and even less in human nature.
I hoped for a long time, then I gave up.
Because as far as I'm concerned, humans are capable of the best and the worst—but when it comes to the worst, they're the best.
So, I'm agnostic by choice and atheist by conviction. Maybe out of intellectual laziness or a lack of spirituality.
Who knows?
On top of that, churches make me uneasy.
That heavy, solemn silence.
The cold stone, the marble that judges you without saying a word.
Stained-glass windows filtering a light loaded with guilt.
All that mysticism is beautiful, and I respect it, but it leaves me cold.
And I'm not alone.
Most French people live split between the altar and the table.
But we have our own pantheon, our own cathedrals. Our pagan temples are restaurants.
They are our refuges and playgrounds where the commandment is simple:
Feast and enjoy yourself.
I am part of that congregation, and I am a devotee.

I work in kitchens five or six days a week, and what do I do on my days off?
I eat in other people's restaurants, like a regular customer. Yeah, I know how it sounds. You've got to be nuts.
But I don't go there just to eat lunch or dinner.
I go the way others go to church—to hear a gospel that resonates deep in my soul and my stomach.
And I absorb that divine melody with delight.
Every dish is a chord.
Every gesture, a note.
Every sip of wine, lyrics.

When I arrive at this place of worship, each time, before entering to receive the homily, I have the same reflex:
I grab the handle, pause for a second, and take a deep breath as if jumping into the void.
The moment I push open the doors of paradise and cross that sacred threshold, a wave of warm air hits me. Scents of wine, worked wood, old leather, and fat.
Life.
The noise welcomes you like a choir of drunken angels, singing something disorderly and chaotic —yet inhabited by an inevitable truth.
The décor takes over:
The gold trim, the wood paneling, the spotted mirrors, and the columns. The worn banquettes and faded velvet chairs.
Further in, the zinc bar pulls you toward an Epicurean communion—one not sealed with the blood of Christ and a paper-thin wafer.

But with peanuts and a glass of red.

Then comes the procession.
Along the way toward the altar, I glance at half-eaten plates and faces glowing with gastronomic ecstasy and mild intoxication. Some laugh. Others exult. But all of them share that same spark—the look of people who know exactly where they are.
In the right place.
Where they belong.
Once seated at the table, I cherish the moment. I take it all in. And at that precise instant, I always think the same thing:
If God exists, he probably has a table reserved in the back, near the radiator, ordering the daily special with a bottle of Burgundy.
Then, once I come back to my senses, he appears.
Right on cue.
Not God... but his deputy.

The Manager.

The guardian of the faith and the rituals.
The one who officiates and blesses the room while he arbitrates the miracles of service.
He walks like a clergyman—slow, observant, and solemn. Hands clasped behind his back with a calm authority, bearing meticulous standards.
Sharp, attentive, and focused.
He is the pope of the house—the only one capable of absolving a customer or excommunicating them.

When he welcomes you, he carries a thick leather-bound book with letters glowing like gold:
The Wine List.
The work of the land and of men.
A miracle made of grapes, rocks, and fruits.
The drink of the gods—a divine alchemy of vines and time that lingers on the tongue like a confession, carrying promises of decadence and intoxication.
Then come the Holy Scriptures.
The psalms of tradition and taste.
For me, it's not a menu; it's a Bible. And I always open it with respect. I read this liturgy of pleasure—its hymns of dishes and sauces—like a printed prayer.
Behind him, an acolyte joins the ceremony.
The devil in an apron arrives.

The Server.

That angel of temptation—a demon whispering in your ear:
"May I suggest a slice of foie gras to start?"
Whether dressed in a white jacket or with a bow tie, he brings the bread and the butter that forgives all sins.
He is the messenger between your appetite and the grace of the kitchen. The one who spreads the chef's gospel.
He recites the specials like a list of deadly sins.
The forbidden fruit—the only thing that makes me believe in humanity again.

And once the missal is in your hand, the healing can begin.
The flock can recite the sacred sermons of gastronomy.
Whether you're a regular or just passing through, make yourself comfortable.
The mass is about to begin.
There are three services a day.
Always at fixed hours.

PS:
For someone who isn't religious, that's quite a lot of liturgical references, no?
All right, it's something to keep an eye on.
I'm just saying—if by the end of this book you find me with my ass in the holy water, chewing on communion wafers...
Then you're allowed to make fun of me.
But only after you've finished your dessert and paid the bill.
In the meantime, I carry on.

When the sun shines

Alright.
I'm going to cool down my delirious, ecumenical psychosis. Let's get back to something more grounded. Less Christ-like.
Let's be serious for a minute.
I love restaurants because they are mirrors of everyday life.
They are open from breakfast to dinner, and if you hang around long enough, you'll see all kinds of people and moods pass through.
Every service has its own vibe, its own rhythm.
And their tiny miracles.
Let's start at the beginning of the day.

Breakfast.

The air is still crisp, and the city is slowly waking up. The street-cleaning trucks wash the pavement while the market stretches out of its cozy nest, setting up its first stalls to welcome the early shoppers.
Terraces unfold to the rhythm of chairs scraping the ground and tables being flipped upright.
There's a strange softness in the air—a charming disorder.
And a curious cast of characters.
You have the night owls soaking up the excesses of the night before with onion soup at dawn.
Businessmen—rarely pleasant at this hour—talking contracts over a parade of empty coffee

cups, a pastry swallowed in three bites, and a briefcase parked at their feet.
You have the regular crowd, enjoying espressos and cafés au lait on the terrace. Chic and practical, because you're shaking off the morning fog while walking the dog.
By the way, if you order a croissant, one of the ends is for the dog. Non-negotiable.
Trust me, you'll be rewarded; the mutt will thank you all day long.
And finally, there's us, the die-hard aficionados. The fallen poets of dawn, looking for inspiration for the day ahead.

You sit down at the table.
From the speakers, the news hums softly—a reassuring background noise that warms the back of your neck.
The tablecloth still carries the crease from being folded; it's spotless and stiff.
Then the server approaches.
He looks good in his uniform. The black vest is spotless; the shirt is slightly wrinkled. The bow tie is a little crooked—just like my brain that very morning. But he looks grumpier than me. One of those damn mornings where we both woke up a bit too late.
Still, I'm instantly won over when I hear his dry, irritated "Bonjour."

You order a coffee, a toast, and a croissant.
The golden triangle.
The Holy Trinity.

The espresso lands on the table. A sharp, nervous, bitter aroma rises from the cup—a captivating and intoxicating fragrance.
Addictive.
At this hour, we don't talk about diets; we're talking about courage. The courage to spread the butter thick. To be generous from the very first slice of baguette.
Because morning truly begins when the crust of the bread gives way—a dry, poetic snap announcing that the day finally has a reason to exist.
The "Échiré" butter doesn't melt—it bends reality. It polishes the world, smooths the edges, repairs the night, and prepares you for your journey.
If the jam spills a little, it doesn't matter; it's the only stain allowed on the tablecloth.
A croissant whispers its crispy layers under your fingers, and you feel that deafening moment of pleasure. You take a bite and wait for the miracle to happen. At that precise second, everything falls back into place.
Because it's not just a breakfast, it's a manifesto of well-being.
You should always start the day with a gesture that lifts you up, that carries you.
Because morning is a promise of happiness, and a good breakfast is a promise kept.
A spark.
The rest doesn't really matter; it can wait.
We'll deal with it later.
The day can begin.

Lunch.

The sun is high and claiming its place, sitting above the rooftops.
The restaurant shakes off its numbness and truly wakes up.
The dining room is set, and stray drafts make the tablecloths dance.
On the table, the glasses are in perfect formation: wine glass, then water glass.
The cutlery is aligned, straight, and proud.
The white napkin, immaculate, sits perfectly centered on the plate, like a salute.
Everything has to be sharp. Impeccable.

The tension is palpable; you can feel it.
Meanwhile, the servers stretch like a squad preparing for battle. They rehearse, warm up, and repeat the specials of the day and the last-minute changes the chef just barked.
They pat their pockets and check their gear.
Wine key, check.
Order pad, check.
Pen, check.
They're up and ready to head to war.
All except for the rookies—pale, trembling at the thought of getting slaughtered in this glorious mess.

While the manager, like a general, walks the room one last time—inspecting the troops and surveying the battlefield. The waiters stand at

attention in a corner, tense and anxious, waiting for the verdict in silence.
As the commander paces the room, they're hoping he doesn't stop. Because if he does, even for a second, you know you're fucked.
You're about to hear about it. You're going to get crushed because your section isn't perfect.

Then comes the order to deploy.
Each server heads to their assigned post.
Every one of them has their favorite or feared section, close to the kitchen or not far enough from it. Which regulars will you get.
They know them by heart.
The ones you dread and try to avoid.
The ones you love to start the day with.
And above all, if there's an upstairs section, you don't want it. In fact, pray that you don't get it.
Because the poor bastard who draws that card—after muttering a final prayer—will be buried under bad jokes and fake condolences.
Everyone laughs.
But no one mocks.
You never know; tomorrow it might be your ass.

Noon sharp.
It's time. The clock strikes like a summons, announcing the imminent chaos.
The doors open, and the first guests arrive.
The pack floods in.
Voices rise and the noise settles in.

Lunch is the pulse of the day. The moment when everything happens. Meetings, deals, reunions, and sometimes comfort are found.
The lunch menu is the pristine definition of democracy.
Everybody can choose between the same three appetizers, three mains, and two desserts.
Everyone gets the same bread, the same wine by the glass, the same price, and the same sunlight through the window.
Or you go rogue.
You defend your own camp by ordering "à la carte," and you eat your own dish at your own pace.

Like every day, the regulars are there, faithful as ever. They have their table, their server, their wine, and their favorite dishes. A choice that will depend on the day, the weather, or their mood—not always forgiving.
The first minutes are crucial; that's when everything locks into place. Because this is the moment when France sits down.
And when France sits down, it orders.
But France is in a hurry, so the service is going to be tight.
During the rush, there is no room for mistakes.
Time to hustle.

In the kitchen,
You go from zero to panic in thirty seconds.
The printer spits tickets at a frantic pace, like a machine gun.

All hands on deck.
The chef barks orders, and the brigade answers in unison in a military crash that shakes the walls.
"Yes, Chef!"
At that hour, everything is critical, including the chef's tolerance for delays.
So you shut up and push plates.
No time to fuck up.
No excuses.
No choice.
No debate.
As service rolls on, the chef drives his troops harder and calls for tables in a state of organized chaos.
In the blink of an eye, the window is jammed, and plates are stacking.
Suddenly, you hear a scream. A howl, sounding like a call from beyond the grave.
"Service, for fuck's sake!"
It's not the moment to test the patience of the chef, as it's running as thin as his taste for kale.
So servers dive for the plates. They sprint, weave, dodge, drop, write, and run back.
Dishes fly out in rhythm.
Trays soar like shields.
Orders rain down like missiles.
The ballet is precise, on the edge of frenzy, but without tension or panic. Just a sense of urgency.
A ruthless efficiency.

In the dining room,
People talk loudly, laugh, eat in a hurry, and sometimes complain.

Usually always the same. The ones you can never please but keep coming back twice a week.
Over time it becomes a routine, a running joke between the three of us; annoying, sure—but familiar.
The client plays it.
The server knows it.
The chef endures it.
We get used to it, and if they don't show up for a few days, we miss them.
At some tables, the butter has already melted into the tray. Sometimes the wine flows; often the sauce shines. But the bread always wipes the plate clean.
A simple gesture.
Ancient.
Almost sacred.
Once their plates are cleared, the guests bless or curse the chef without naming him. The one who never comes out among mortals, yet whose presence is always felt—walled off in his kitchen. Because of him, taste is celebrated without dogma or prayer. A communion through the mouth and the stomach.
Toward the end of lunch, some guests glance at their watches and treat themselves.
"Hey, I've got time for dessert."
Or:
"Bring me another espresso."

As for the servers, there is no need to check the clock.

Around two PM, you turn around... and the room is empty. Everyone vanished at once, like a tide pulling back brutally.
As if... evaporated.
After the roaring din comes a staggering silence.
The service is over.
Still, a few stragglers remain, lingering over a digestif. They talk shop, vacations, and politics.
At the next table, some passersby stretch the moment, holding onto a sliver of happiness while waiting for the rain to stop.
In the back, a couple of tourists watch this circus, stunned and impressed by the madness. Like children staring at a magic trick they don't understand.

The head waiters are out of breath, sweating bullets while clearing tables.
The dishwashers are buried under a mountain of glasses, cutlery, and plates.
Slowly, the dining room straightens itself up after the storm.
Calm returns.
Serenity too.

For the staff, this is the moment of grace.
The reward after the chaos.
A tight espresso, a cigarette on the sidewalk, and laughter.
Because now—finally—you can spit out all the bullshit you've been choking on for the past three hours.

When the night falls

The day slowly fades.
The restaurant's dim light falls over the tablecloths like a caress.
Once the cutlery has been polished anew, the staff finishes setting the tables.
A candle reflects in the glassware, making it sparkle—a flame that adds sensuality to the moment.
A warm, festive hum settles into the air. A hushed, friendly mood takes hold.
The atmosphere has shifted.
The lights are softer now, and the dining room regains its elegance. Everything feels slower, gentler.
Intimate.
The place has shed its skin and reclaimed its mystery.
Wine will replace coffee, and the din will turn into a murmur.

The opening crew is gone.
They'll eat dinner with family or friends. Maybe in front of the TV, in good company. Couples will recount their day—the annoying customers, the lunch rush, the clash with the manager, and the clash with that stubborn bastard of a chef.
Some servers on split shifts are already there.
They wipe away fatigue with the back of a towel; the lunch battle left its marks.

They'll work part of the service before heading home, drained, legs heavy, and feet sore.
But with the satisfaction of a job well done.
At home, the first reflex is to pour a drink, then grab a quick bite, eaten on the corner of a table.
Finally able to enjoy a brief moment of calm.

Others have arrived.
The closing crew, the night birds.
Fresh—well, not always.
Sometimes already a little loosened and buzzed up by a late lunch that ran a bit wetter than usual.
But rested.
Ready to suggest.
To tempt.
Because dinner is the return of seduction.
Now there's time to enchant the guests and to sing the praises of the specials. To sell a dish properly and talk about seasonal vegetables.
To linger over terroirs and to praise a wine.
To whisper an aperitif or a digestif.

It's seven o'clock.
It's the moment to welcome those leaving their homes or arriving straight from work.
It's no longer just a meal; it's a story at each table.
A story of people, laughter, pleasure, heartache, and sometimes silence.
The doors open, and the first evening guests arrive, still wrapped in their coats.
You can smell the crispness of the cold and measure the weight of the day still hanging from their shoulders.

You sense the joy or the tension they carry with them—it will set the tone for the entire evening.
There are those meeting friends, settling in for a long night of laughter and the occasional arguments.
The lovers. Speaking softly. Smiling. Declaring their feelings through knowing glances.
First dates, where you seduce, flirt, and where hands brush against each other by accident.
And the last ones, where you cry and console each other, where words are scarce and awkward silences do most of the heavy lifting.
There are the solitary ones too.
Taking their time and using the dining room as a refuge from loneliness.
And sometimes, in a corner, a hard-working soul thinking deeply catches a spark of inspiration and scribbles it down in a notebook.

When the server approaches the table, he is more composed now—confident and reassuring.
The tie is back in place, neatly adjusted; the tone of his voice is steady, calm, almost comforting.
Because now we're no longer talking about productivity; we're talking about desire.
As the night is just beginning, dinner is the return of pleasure.
Dishes are described like poems.
Appetizers and desserts become a luxury again.
Wine, a balm.
Butter, an excuse.

In the kitchen, the brigade finally breathes.

The dining room is full, but the service flows. Orders arrive at regular intervals, overlapping smoothly instead of piling up.
Gestures are precise: you flambé, you plate, and you taste.
The chef no longer shouts; he orchestrates.
He conducts.
Pots and pans no longer clash; they sing.
It's different music, another tempo.
The time of mastery, of control.

Meanwhile, the dining room grows confidential. You hear discreet laughter, the clink of glasses, and sometimes the soft, muffled pop of a champagne cork.
Some glances meet; others turn away.
The restaurant becomes a theater of half-spoken words, suspended promises, or sharp reproaches. This is France at its long dinners, where bottles empty too quickly and conversations reshape the world. Often rounded off with one last coffee.
Or a small digestif.
But why *small?*

Little by little, the last glasses empty, and the sections thin out. One couple still lingers, fingers intertwined above an empty plate.
The manager checks his watch, and the servers stack the menus. They yawn discreetly, as their patience thins as the hours stretch on.
The light dims further; the last guests call for the check and drift away.

The chairs and tables are empty now—but traces remain.
Whiffs of wine and browned butter.
Wilted bouquets on the tables, defeated by the air-conditioning or the heat.
A lipstick mark on a glass.
Stained napkins, casually left behind like rumpled clothes tossed on the floor.
The tablecloth is wrinkled—like the sheet of an unmade bed after a passionate embrace.
A fragrance of desire still hangs in the air.
The scent of pleasure.

The lights come back up, and the staff blink, slightly dazzled. They step out of the dimness of performance and come back into the clarity of reality.
The manager heads to the office to count the till and write the night's report.
The team—having folded the tablecloths and blown out the candles—sits down at the bar with the bartender for one last drink.
One last smile.
One last cigarette.
Then everyone leaves.
The lights go out.
The dining room falls asleep.
Gently.
And somewhere, behind a swinging door, a single light remains on. And one man stands alone in his sanctuary.

The chef.

He puts away his knives.
Everything is clean.
He finishes his glass of wine while looking at his kitchen with love and respect.
He checks the orders. The fridges.
Before he steps out, he contemplates his silent kitchen. A discreet smile, filled with gratitude, appears on his face. And with a quiet pride in his eyes, he whispers:
"See you tomorrow."
Once outside, the city has grown cold again, but deep inside him burns an invisible fire.
An untamable flame.
The satisfaction of knowing he gave pleasure through skills and craft.
Through dishes, some made in a rush, some in frustration, and others by habit. But always made with love.
Once again, the priest of food has delivered his sermon and pulled off his miracle;
Offering a suspended moment in the day of his parishioners.
Those who came seeking consolation and comfort.
Those who came to confess their hunger.
Those who came to commune with fate or atone for a day.
And those who came to celebrate a victory or bury a sorrow.

The day is over.
Ite, missa est.

The mass is finished.
Lights out.

DNA

You don't become a server, a cook, a bartender, or a chef by accident.
You become one by instinct, by a crack in the armor, by necessity, and by passion.
Most of the time by love... but never out of spite.
And you stick with it because you have something to prove or something to run from.
To escape.
It's a path, an initiation. A life choice.

Have you heard the old line by Jean Anthelme Brillat-Savarin?
"Tell me what you eat, and I'll tell you who you are."
Well, in hospitality, we have another one—one that is universal, brutal, but undisputed.
"Tell me where you work, and I'll tell you who you are."
Because the place shapes the person.
A bistro, a brasserie, a café, or a fine-dining restaurant aren't just different kitchens.
They're different worlds, different speeds, and different ways of existing.
The people who work there don't carry themselves the same way. They don't speak the same language and don't even breathe the same.
Their clothes, their eyes, the way they say "chef" or "good evening, sir or madam."
Everything gives away the world they belong to or work in.

And you don't enter those worlds by chance.

There are the bistro people:
Fast, sharp, a little rogue. A bit rough around the edges. Always a rag and a nasty joke within reach
The brasserie crew:
Lunchtime and dinnertime warriors. Solid, relentless—built to serve two hundred and fifty covers without blinking and breaking a sweat.
Then the café missionaries:
The tray grinders, gladiators of the espresso and the sandwich, and the hot chocolate on a rainy day.
And finally, the monk-soldiers of fine dining: precise, silent, and inhabited by perfection like a curse.
Some need the surgical order of fine dining.
Others thrive in the flavorful chaos of a bistro.
Some enjoy the daily marathon of the café.
And others can only breathe in the crooked yet organized choreography of the brasserie.
A bistro teaches you resourcefulness and how to hustle through mayhem.
A brasserie teaches endurance and style.
A café teaches you survival and the art of wading through reality.
Fine dining lets you taste the sweetness of excellence or the bitterness of the fall.
Four temples.
Four liturgies.
But one single rule.
Serve, give pleasure, and hold the line until the end of service.

And then, do it again.

Everyone chooses a side. And sometimes, the side chooses you. Because let's be clear, you don't move through these worlds the way you cross a street. And you don't change like you change shirts.
Because in the middle of all this mess, you build yourself an identity.
You rub against it and get burned by it.
You reveal yourself there, and you live inside it.
And at the end of the road, everything has changed.
Your walk.
Your voice.
Your gaze.
You're not looking at the world the same way.
Because deep down, in restaurants, you're not just serving food.
You're serving who you are.
You're serving your nature, your character.
That's something no school will ever teach you.
The field shapes you, and what makes you stay is the DNA.
The rest is irrelevant.
Details and bullshit stories—you tell yourself to avoid facing reality. To keep you believing you can quit whenever you want.
Well, you can't.
Trust me, I tried.
But it comes back to haunt you like a bad dream.
We are adrenaline junkies, and this job is our drug.

We need our daily fix.
We can't live without it.

I like to compare restaurants to wild animals: ruthless, challenging, demanding, and complex. They have a soul, a heart, a brain, and a belly. and they breathe, and their vital organs need fuel, air, and blood.
So I invite you to get up close and personal.
Sniff those beasts.
A kind of medical examination.
But before we start the check-up, we're going to walk around the premises. Because you need to know where you're stepping into—and what surrounds you.
We are going to dissect them.
Species by species.
Organ by organ.
So put on your camouflage. We are going to enter into their hunting grounds and, above all, see how they defend them.
We're heading right into their dens.

No bullshit
No filters.
But maybe a hint of poetry.

Fine dining

In haute gastronomy, the dining room is beautiful and elegant.
Plush. Refined. But discreet enough not to distract you from the real reason you came there.
To forget the noise of your everyday life and find the promises of transcendence.
And nothing must interfere with the experience.
That is why there is barely any music.
No distraction; just enough welcoming warmth to calm you down, to put you in the right condition.
So consider it as an airlock.
A buffer zone between the gates of heaven and the Garden of Eden.

The staff is flawless.
Precise, knowledgeable, present yet withdrawn.
Always one step back—like a shadow that knows exactly when to appear and when to vanish.
Posture is upright, serious, and sometimes borderline rigid, because service codes here are anything but flexible.
They serve the guest, but their true role is to put the kitchen in the spotlight.
They are the velvet case around a jewel. the frame that makes the stone shine.
And even if the front and back of house walk together on the path toward the divine—inseparable, dependent on each other—they are not quite equals.

Everything needs to be perfect, but the kitchen is the one with the checkmate move.

Which brings us to the brigade.

What a fascinating species—these pioneers of gastronomy.
Mystics of sauce.
Psychotics of molecules.
Neurotics of emulsions.
These illuminated souls enlist in this regiment the way others go on crusade, wielding tweezers like swords and pristine towels like shields.
Their quest for the Holy Grail is absolute harmony. The perfect plate.
These stealthy ninjas, with surgical movements and razor-precise cuts, are like elite troops fueled by the amphetamines of creativity.
Most of them think longer about a carrot than some people do about their future. They speak of an onion as if it were a poem and see a metaphysic in a sauce that is completely incomprehensible to us, mere mortals.
These mathematicians of taste create dishes the way others solve equations. They calibrate, count, and dress plates like a theorem.
None of them think—they're inhabited. Possessed.
They spend entire nights on a juice, weeks on a single recipe.
They are more than cooks; they are architects of the palate—builders of emotion, erecting edible cathedrals.

In their world, everything is timing and tension.
Concept and analysis.
They explore and sublimate; their kitchen is a particle accelerator. They don't season—they release aromas and provoke flavors. And it comes down to the grain of salt.
These mad scientists know it.
Because they've counted them all, like an astronomer counts the stars. And in their galaxy, there's only one constellation that obsesses them: the Michelin kind.

The service.

In a fine-dining kitchen, service unfolds in apnea and silence.
You don't breathe.
You don't speak.
At best, you whisper.
Sometimes, you may suggest.
Every service is an exploration, a dive into the depths of excellence.
All of it under the eye of a Cerberus on the brink of a burnout.

The chef.

Talented. Brilliant. Creative.
But he is crushed between the fear of disappointment, his own ego, and the pursuit of the sublime—opposite forces that compress him, torture him, and spin him in a centrifuge.

Because the slightest mistake, the smallest approximation, is a ticking time bomb.
He's not an idealist; he's a dreamer. And a compulsive gambler.
He bets his life on every menu, wagering everything on each silence, each smile in the dining room, hoping he's finally found the winning formula.
And when everything aligns... when everything is in place. When the plate leaves the pass at the exact second...
It's perfect.
Millimeter-precise and immaculate.
A masterpiece.
It's the jackpot.
But when he draws the wrong number, this art destroys as much as it elevates. It eats your life and twists your brain. It shreds your nerves and replaces laughter with precision and conviviality with control.
You think only of reviews, rankings, and guides. About what others think. Scores.
Numbers that haunt you and build or wreck a lifetime of sacrifice and labor in a New York minute.

And me, in all that...
As I've already said in my previous book, fine dining is not my thing. I never felt comfortable there. Even at the time I was front of house, whether as a server or a manager. I wasn't in my place.

And now that I'm in the kitchen, nothing has changed.
Not for me.
I've been offered chef positions in starred restaurants. I always refused. Not for lack of ambition, but because I couldn't breathe there.
Not even as a guest.
Standing in silent awe in front of a plate bores me to death.
Why spend three hours dissecting a dish?
Leave it the fuck alone, eat it, and enjoy it.
Plus, the whole ceremony in the dining room exhausts me.
The rigidity.
The constraints.
The codes.
I don't like eating in whispers, and I hate being watched at every bite. Even more being judged if I drop my fork.

Let me tell you a story that says a lot about fine dining... and about me.
I'm not too proud of it, but what the hell.
A long time ago, one day, I was eating in one of those Michelin-starred temples.
I sat down, and the head waiter brought the bread.
Like an idiot, I ask for butter.
I swear, I thought he was going to shit himself.
He looked at me like some Neanderthal caveman.
Witnessing his exasperation lit my fuse.
Because I'm an asshole by nature, and purely out of provocation, I added—just to finish him off:

"If you don't have butter, mayonnaise will do..."
That was it.
It was not very charitable, I know.
But I couldn't help it. I just couldn't fucking help it.
Besides, he started it.

All of which is to say, it's not my world; it doesn't fit my DNA.
Even the way the dining room staff speak to guests, or to each other... I'd stick out like a sore thumb.
Because I wear insolence like a badge and rebellion like a banner. My big mouth as a shield and stupidity as a religion. I'm too rough. Too raw. Too primitive.
So no, I never belonged in culinary school, and even less in these temples of perfection.
My quest is at the bottom of a saucepan; I taste with a spoon and adjust by instinct. I love kitchens with organized chaos, and being on the edge of fury inspires me. I like noise. Commotion, camaraderie, and above all, simplicity.
Simple wines.
Simple dishes.
Simple people.
Fine dining is pure genius, like a symphony or an opera.
I prefer rock and roll.
And I have way too much fun cooking for people who eat with their fingers and mop up the sauce with bread...and a bit of butter.

That one's for him—just in case he recognizes himself.

Still... Justice must be done, and credit is due.
I admire them because I love talent.
Especially the kind I don't have.
And that, I respect.
Those magnificent chefs and cooks, inspired, brilliant, and complex, are artists chasing eternity on a plate.
And when it's beautiful, it's unique.
When it's precise, it's a technical orgasm. Visceral. Guttural.
But I don't envy them.
They have nobility and elegance, without a doubt.
Technique, for sure.
The respect and admiration of the profession, undeniably.
But conviviality?
What about dripping fat and overflowing laughter?
Stupidity, shits, and giggles?
Have you noticed? In fine dining, people smile, admire, and whisper.
But in a bistro or a brasserie...people laugh out loud and bump into each other.
It's alive. It swarms.

So while haute gastronomy reaches the stars, others prefer to keep their feet on the ground. Because fine dining may be the culinary summit, but it's also where you suffocate if you run out of air.

And between the two... I chose.
I chose oxygen.
I chose a restaurant where wine flows and meals are eaten without a dissertation.
Where servers wear a towel on their belt and call you by your first name with a biting smile—fueled By a shining irony and sharp sarcasm.
A counter, a daily special, and a glass of house wine.
Staff who laugh, who argue, who cook the way you love a woman.
Without restraint.
Without codes.
Without formalities.
I need a place where no one weighs the salt or happiness.
Where the only timing that matters is the time for a shot and a slice of pâté.
And if I'm expected to be on the battlefield, I'd rather not wear a tuxedo. But a pair of jeans and sneakers. Balls out and my knife between my teeth. Yeah. Like a pirate.
But also where there's still bearing, tradition, and "savoir-faire."
And that place.
That kingdom.
That France... It is the brasserie.

The Brasseries

Here, we're no longer in the clouds or those high spheres where oxygen runs thin. We leave the kingdom of the gods and enter royalty.
This is the heart of France.
Beyond the starred temples exists a world ruled by its own very specific decorums. A place where everything blends without betraying itself.
Flawless cuisine, noise, joy, and wine.
Fatigue and grace.
Tradition and discipline of service.
This is a stronghold with a backbone—a perfect balance of glorious mess and grandeur.
A sacred bridge between molecular cuisine and beef bourguignon.
Middle Earth, but with more butter.
Neither snobbish nor trendy.
Neither nostalgic nor arrogant.
And never outdated.
Just there, standing on its pedestal, vividly alive and vibrant.
It's a place everyone eventually comes back to.
The old to remember, the young to learn, and the rest is simply to eat well.
All French people still lunch and dine there with a light heart because we trust these defenders of an honest and uncompromising cuisine.
You might see a cabinet minister or a delivery guy.
An actress or a truck driver.
A family dinner or a business meal.

And no one looks down on you.

From the outside, the sign is impossible to miss—elegant, flowing lettering, like a perfectly reduced sauce.
Inside, the décor is charming, slightly bourgeois, but just enough.
Under your feet, worn carpet that slowly destroys the servers' feet.
On the walls, faded tapestries depict hunting scenes and forest beasts.
On the ceiling, light fixtures yellowed by life—by years of cigarettes and ten thousand services that left their mark.
Not to mention the wood paneling and the vinyl banquettes that smell of yesteryear. A light rancid scent, yet elegant. Almost divine.
It carries me away with every breath—the noble perfume of houses that have lived and sweated.
Pure happiness, really.

Service is a disciplined chaos, a perfect choreography.
A mix of disruptions, order, and style.
Everything moves, everything trembles; it all hangs by a thread... but nothing breaks.
Here we serve fast and the old-fashioned way, and the ramparts of this fortress are the front-of-house staff.
A tribe of their own.
Not the lofty artists of fine dining, but soldiers of noon and midnight. A well-drilled army, proud of its history, wearing the name of the house like a

flag. Square and efficient, with just enough madness to keep it all afloat.

The bartender

If there's one sacred figure in a brasserie, it's him. Behind his bar, he listens without asking. Advises without judging. Serves without measuring.
He knows who drinks to celebrate and who drinks to forget. Who drinks just to stay on the edge of sobriety, just to hold themselves together, or to atone for something.
The bar is a confessional for heretics and hedonists.
Leaning on the zinc, sitting on a stool, or standing, you lay down your guard, your fears, and your hopes. Your tiny victories and your huge failures. Your loneliness and your breakups.
Secrets and confessions even priests don't hear anymore.
And he stays there, unshaken, always polishing his glasses.
Don't be mistaken. That gesture is how he absolves us.
At the bar, you don't really talk to the bartender. You talk to yourself.
He's just the discreet witness of our existence.

The Chef.

Often a defector from fine dining—a battle-scarred veteran of the stoves. A man trained in beautiful gestures, millimeter-perfect plating, and

high ceremony. But he found a second wind in this kitchen, where he can breathe and express himself. He cooks delicate and soulful meals without the suffocating pressure of Michelin stars. Not to seduce a critic, but to be true to himself and to nourish.
He's a battered general of rushes and fire, holding his brigade with a firm hand and his menu close to his heart. And his guts.
A historian of flavor, who knows sauces like others know scripture.
An archaeologist of butter, who respects flame, fat, and the taste of France.
Not a tortured artist, but a magnificent craftsman.
A chef in love with a culinary tradition still blazing with truth.
Such as....

The server

Not everyone signs up for a brasserie. It's a specific universe.
You chose this path like entering a seminary.
Ad vitam æternam.
This giant of service wears his white jacket tall and proud, like a symbol of resistance.
He knows the menu by heart and the wine list down to the vintage. He's flawless on the daily specials. He knows the music by heart.
And the kitchen brigade.
He speaks to them as an equal because he respects their labor and their sacrifices.

They all share the same demand for the rigor of the service.
The same respect for the dish.
The effort.
The nobility of the craft.
He carves a côte de bœuf table-side and fillets a sole meunière blindfolded.
Even the chef can only bow to this heroic and distinguished knight—the guardian of a house full of history, of a clan.

When he crosses the dining room during service at a frantic pace, his step is measured. The shirt is soaked, and eyes are on the prize.
He's the only one who sees you when you think no one's watching. He observes everything.
He reads a table before the guest even sits down.
He senses The moods, the hungers, the thirsts, the tempers.
Faces. Silences. Looks.
Couples forming and falling apart.
Awkward beginnings, endings that hurt, and silences that scare.
Smiles that mean maybe tonight and looks that say never again.
Forced laughter and discreet tears.
Ruined birthdays.
Successful proposals and poorly hidden affairs.
First and last times.
He respects as much the loners talking to their wine as the gathering of friends laughing too loud.

The server is the witness to our lives, watching them pass without lingering too long on any single one. Including his own.
His life runs like a river, between tables, against time.
The time between courses.
The time left before the next service.

Please, allow me an aside—to you who work in brasseries, front and back of house.
You, who, every lunch and dinner, give us a concert of humanism where everyone knows their note, their tempo, and their style.
Thank you. Thank you for this poetry of urgency.
Brutal.
Sublime.
Authentic.
Even if words fall short of my respect, my gratitude, and my admiration. Let's try anyway.
I love you.
Like family.
But I have to tell you, your little cousins worry me. You know the ones... the little punks. The rascals. Those unruly cherubs who think they're rebels.

Ladies and gentlemen, hospitality is one big family. But to understand this great tribe, we need to go back to our x-ray of the industry.
We've already put the head and brain through the scanner.
Fine dining.
The kingdom of ideas and obsessions,

Where everything is calculated, conceptualized, doubted, and sometimes hallucinated.
Where genius flirts with madness and perfection brushes up against exhaustion.
We examined the heart.
The brasserie.
That tireless engine. That warm pulse that keeps France on its feet.
Alive. Vibrant.
And now...
We're going to dive into the belly of the beast.
The intestines.
The stomach.
The liver.

And that popular place.
Essential.
Irreplaceable.

It's the bistro.

The Bistrot

Alright. Now we're home.
My place.
My sandbox.
Quicksand, sure, because it's a total mud pit.

The bistro is the neighborhood's belly.
Where everything gets eaten, drunk, and digested with taste and humor. But with very little mercy.
Where everything transforms, stories of good days and shitty ones.
It's the truancy version of hospitality.
No protocol and no instruction manual.
No rules.
No stars.
Just guts and chaos.
A place where memory catches fire and a sanctuary for the hungry-for-life and the thirsty-for-pleasure.
But before we talk about staff and service, we need to set the scene.

You recognize the local bistro before you even walk in.
The façade isn't extraordinary—a faded sign, warm colors, and bold letters.
On the windows, traces of words erased by time and winter fog.
And often, a terrace.
On the wall, a menu.
Where you find dishes that warm the soul.

Celeriac remoulade, house-made country pâté, and leeks vinaigrette.
Beef and carrots, coq au vin, and an andouillette.
A cheese plate, a crème caramel, and a floating island.
Recipes that smell like love, raw honesty, and tenderness. Gluttony and pleasure.
Oldies but goodies.

On the sidewalk, a chalkboard that's still standing by pure miracle, with the daily special written in chalk. Calligraphed by the least bad of us. It's rarely the kitchen, as we write like trolls. Most of the time, it's the hostess or a waitress.
On it, braised beef cheek, house mashed potatoes, Endive and ham gratin. A garlic salted cod brandade.
That's it.
No storytelling. No need for a text explanation.
Simple cooking and honest feeding.
It goes down smooth, and it hits the spot.

Inside, it's a treasure.
You walk in without a reservation, and you leave the bullshit on at the door.
Immediately, you are grabbed by the smell of butter sizzling and meat browning. Roasted garlic and parsley freshly chopped with a knife.
You're catapulted right back into childhood.
Then the counter,
Where the children of the zinc kill time without wasting it, over a plate of cold cuts and a glass of red.

You reach the dining room; it's packed and loud... ready to explode.
The wooden chairs are a little old, sticky, shaky, and tired—they've carried everyone.
Couples. Friends. Workers.
The lost. The found.
The "I don't know where the fuck I am, but, hell, I'm good here."
They've seen it all. And if they could talk, they'd have stories for days.
Tables are small, tight, and sometimes wobbly.
But this little corner of a table is worth more than a thousand trendy spots.
On it, no white linen, just paper and napkins that have lived.
Duralex glasses clinking and ringing like the bells of paradise.
Water carafes from another time and wine pitchers working the line, filling and emptying on an endless loop.
In this mess, everything is cramped ... except the people, the food, the wine, and the laughter.
It's a time capsule that transports you to a time where old recipes rub shoulders with drunkenness, hangovers, and cheeky talk.
That's the décor.

Now, the kitchen crew.

Bad boys.
The ones at school who sat in the back row, by the heater.

To work in a bistro, you need very specific qualities.
Cold blood.
A sharp, second-degree sense of humor.
And the ability to thrive in chaos.
That's where you find weirdos like me.
Hard-working, stubborn, and rough.
Eccentric, some might say erratic
And above all, we suffer from a pathological allergy to authority.
That's why we're built for the bistro—and nowhere else.
Fine dining? We'd last an hour.
Brasserie? Maybe two.
Why?
Uniforms? Meh. Not our thing.
Chef's hats? Go fuck yourself.
Weighing things, following a recipe?
Sure. Except I don't have a scale, and I don't have time to read. Anyway, I only trust my eyes, my nose, and my tongue.
Beat it.
When we make a daily special, you're not talking food-and-wine pairings. We're talking hunger.
Cravings.
We reduce by feel and taste with our fingers. And we work to the sound of the world around us.
We're a tribe of lunatics for whom presentation is secondary. It has to be clean and appetizing, of course. But above all, it has to smell good and taste good.
Bottom line, we're a gang of idealistic, gentle maniacs who still believe a well-executed dish and

a glass of house wine can save the day of a perfect stranger.

The service

Same thing.
Pure rock 'n' roll.
The server knows everyone. Or pretends to.
Uses first names, jokes around, offers coffees, and talks bullshit between two digestifs.
He listens. He consoles, and he's not shy to share his own troubles too.
He's a priest without a cassock—a bright, defrocked cleric who hears confessions between glasses of wine. And grants absolution between shepherd's pie and rum baba.

Speaking of which, here's the ultimate test to know if you're in a serious place.
If you order a rum baba and the rum isn't already on the plate, but it arrives in a bottle placed on the table next to your dessert.
Then you know.
You're in good hands.
It's the motherland.

In a bistro, you can arrive alone and leave with company.
Because here, no one judges you.
When we talk to you, we look you in the eye.
When we serve you, we smile at you.
And when you eat, we nourish you.
And you always leave a little less empty.

A little better than when you came in.

So I get irritated when I see the bistro evolving, “modernizing.”
It doesn’t get rougher. It gets noble and trendy.
Even worse—it gets conceptual. On the plate and on the scene.
Alright, here I go, making friends again... Let's talk about *bistronomy*.
That cute new invention hailed as a so-called modern philosophy. A cult where fashionable urbanites gather around gluten-free beef bourguignon—without the beef. Washing it down with “zero additives” wines, what the snobs call non-chaptalized bottles.
Regarding the menu, between the technical spec sheets and the complete surrender to the wellness gurus, the food turned bland.
Boring.
The dining room?
The server is a hipster, an organic wine salesman, vaping between two sips of “smart water” in a recycled, low-carbon-footprint plastic bottle.
Crap, since when did the bistro become so sterile?

Okay.
I calm down.
I can get loud and run hot. On a short fuse. But I love these places too much to watch them get gutted in silence.
So yes, sometimes I spill over. I color outside the lines a little.

But I stay optimistic, because thankfully, there are still die-hards hanging around.

The last romantics.
Battered old-timers and young ones who still believe.
Servers with loud mouths and stained aprons, greeting regulars by their first name.
They spread butter with a trowel and pour wine by sight. Always to the rim. Cooks, stubborn enough to measure by eye and serve by ladle.
They work on instinct, not on an algorithm.
All of them talk about fat, cooking, time, terroir, and loyal customers—not visibility or branding.
They are the guardians of the fire.
They're holding the line against trends and influencers. They know taste can't be digitized; it cannot be "liked." And that pleasure isn't shared in "stories" but at the table.
And as long as there's a bistro that smells like onion, roasted coffee, and red wine,
As long as a customer stands up to say,
"Thanks, that was fucking awesome."
Then all is not lost.
It's a breath of fresh air, and a good thing too, because we're going to need it.

We're about to hit the lung of France.
The kingdom of croque-monsieur and pinball.
The temple of ham-and-salted butter sandwiches and the "grand crème."
Goddamn, just saying the name gives me chills.

The cafés.

The Cafés

Alright, if you're French, brace yourself because we're taking a trip down memory lane.
If not, I welcome you to the golden age of our teenage years, when our world was still ruled by cafés.
But I'm not talking about a cup of Joe, but a French joint.
What's the difference? It has a certain...how do you say? A certain "je ne sais quoi."
You guys kill me when I hear you use this expression. Nobody in French says that, because it makes no fucking sense at all.
Food for thought: if you're ever tempted to use it, make sure there are no frogs around you to hear you.
Anyway.
I need to add a crucial bit of precision.
They are very different from the ones you have here in the U.S.;
We call them "un troquet."
Humble.
Rough.
Human.
Organic.
Visceral.
Not the sanitized, trendy, hip places where you gather to order a smoothie or a croissant with ham and cheese.
By the way, you will never find those in France.

So if one day you go there. Never, ever, under no circumstances, ask for it; it's a red flag.
It's not a goddamn sandwich, for fuck's sake.
It has never been and never will be.
You will find yourself in a standoff with the owner of the shop, or at the very least, witness a sardonic smile from the person sitting next to you.
Same thing in Italy: never ask for a cappuccino in the middle of the day.
Those items are for breakfast.
ONLY.
Now that I have this weight off my chest, I feel better. I have been dying to say this for twenty years. Now let's get back to the heart of the matter.

You could not find a set that is more used in the history of French cinema.
And there's a reason for that.
If there are cathedrals—restaurants for special occasions—there are also churches for everyday mass. They are everywhere in France, in the cities, suburbs, and small villages.
The bar-tabac PMU. The local dive.
It is the nervous system and the lung of everything that moves in towns, middle-of-nowhere corners, and forgotten places.
And here, nothing is hidden; it is glassed in like an aquarium of the ordinary. Everyday life is on display—boring, sad, joyful, or stubbornly normal.

The facade?

A sign from another era, lit by a pale white neon. Next to it, a loud red diamond, reminding you they sell cigarettes. That old symbol of rebellion, now ostracized by the wellness ayatollahs.

Inside,
The counter where you rest your elbow is littered with discarded scratch-off tickets—left there by occasional gamblers abandoned by both hope and luck.
Back in the day, that very same counter held hard-boiled eggs and peanut dispensers.
All erased from the picture by fanatical hygienist dictators in the name of a narrow, self-righteous morality.
Crap. I've jumped the tracks again. My bad; I'll stay on topic.
Behind the bar, an old coffee machine—tired of frothing milk—grumbles and spits steam with metallic rattling. Besides it, stacked glasses and liquor bottles of some brands that don't even exist anymore.

And then, you have the owners.

The innkeepers of the ordinary.
Him—jokes locked and loaded in a holster, ready to draw, always with a glass within reach.
Her—she sighs every time her other half calls a "round on the house" because she's usually the one who does the books. And she's exhausted from pretending to laugh at the same jokes for the past twenty years.

They know everything, every secret.
The debts.
The affairs.
The grudges.
As for the regulars, some don't even have to order.
a smile, and an "As usual."
A nod, and it's poured.

Here comes the server.

Like the baguette, the beret, and the Eiffel Tower, he is one of the most vivid Parisian icons.
For us, he's the definitive French antihero.
A servant of the fleeting, a master of the order-on-the-go. A tray marathoner, who has change stuffed into his vest pockets and the wine key chained at the belt. He is a blur of motion because there is always one more customer. He stacks drinks like a circus juggler. And it fits, because here, there are clown acts. Sometimes poetic, other times...merely pathetic.
Every café has its apostles, its penitents, its saints, its devils, and its lost souls.
Morning workers grabbing an espresso at the counter.
Retirees reminiscing about the good old days, bitching that everything is going down the drain.
Teenagers reshaping the world, or drunks quietly collapsing.
And those who come back to life after work, over a small glass of house white.
Sometimes some passerby shelters from the rain with a hot chocolate.

In winter, the fogged-up windows isolated from the world those standing at the bar while eating a sandwich with a name that sounds like a postcard and defines an identity.
"The Parisian."
"The Lyonnais."
"The Auvergnat."
It's the only place where people share without knowing each other. And if you listen closely and carefully to the conversations, when those tongues loosen, poetry takes off. All in a language whose pauses, rambles, anger, laughter, and silences cement a country and give depth to the insignificant.

I still remember the café of my teenage years. Where I spent my youth, where I blew my pocket money.
A place of first laughs, first flirts, and first tilts. It was where I smoked my first cigarettes and learned the meaning of freedom. It shaped my identity, my insults, and my jokes.
In high school, I'd wake up early just to meet the guys before class. The night before, we'd call each other to say that magic sentence:
"See you tomorrow at the café."
No GPS. No bullshit Zoom meetings.
Those magic winter mornings in Paris, you were coming out of the subway into a freezing rain. But when you pushed the door open, at the risk of shocking you, that suspended haze that filled our lungs smelled like a full ashtray and pastis.
Well, it calmed us.

Because it was the scent of our refuge, where we were free to be ourselves, without the overwhelming shadow of our parents.

Once inside, we scanned the room to find our crew. As we walked to the table, we felt the first thrills of the day. That electric moment when you kissed hello a girl from class you were crazy about while pretending not to care.
You had to play it cool.
Sitting around a “kawa” (our slang for an espresso), we reviewed the night's events:
The erotic movie we caught on TV at eleven p.m.
Unfinished homework.
The math test we hadn't studied for.
We masterminded our next scores—forging a parent’s signature on a bad report card.
That moment was our Instagram Reel.
Our Facebook story.

At noon, we’d bolt from school, and the question always popped: Who are we hanging with today? Every group had its café, and you never changed. Ever. You chose it based on the pinball machines, the jukebox, and—above all—the girls. When crews mixed, there were endless arguments over where to eat, but in the end, everyone retreated to their own café with their own folks.
Nobody likes change. Especially teenagers.

At the start of the school year, we were nervous and shy. We didn’t know the server’s name, so we approached with careful politeness:

“Garçon, s'il vous plaît.”
Three months later, we walked in like conquerors.
We greeted the server like VIPs in a nightclub.
We’d sit down, saving seats for the stragglers:
“Hey Jerome, two Cokes and a croque!”
Always checking to see if we’d impressed the girls.
Morons.

Once seated, we emptied our pockets and counted our change. We had to split the loot between food, drinks, and pinball.
Between bites of a sandwich, we rushed the machine like starving animals. We acted tough. Street badasses. When in reality, we were just pimply idiots from nice neighborhoods.
We took turns playing—one of us showing off with fake confidence while the others scanned the girls to see if they were watching. If we caught an eye, we reached for our lethal weapon.
We saved one last coin for the dedication.
At the jukebox, we picked the song she liked or the one we thought fit the vibe.
Then the speakers blasted a hit in a magical cacophony of the sound from a shitty old speaker, pinball bells, and ambient chaos.
We looked over our shoulders, anxious, with sweaty palms. If she smiled, we knew we had a shot.
Today, you’d say, “I got a like.”
Back then, it was either glory or a total FUBAR rejection.
God, we were idiots. But it was touching.
Those were the good times.

That was our world.
A universe codified with its own markers and rituals. The underage cocktails: Mint Diabolo. Strawberry milk. Grenadine.
Sometimes you crossed from adolescence into adulthood just by pushing that door. We played grown-ups without being them. We drank Monacos and panachés, served in sticky glasses we could barely finish because they were disgusting. But we choked them down anyway. Because she was watching.
Everything tasted of carelessness and transgression.
We hung around the café to delay the inevitable. Because after that, we knew the party was over. Responsibilities. Work. Bills.

And unfortunately, I can confirm it.
The party is over; it's a new game now.
On a trip back to Paris, I went looking for that spirit. To remember. To reminisce.
Well, imagine my surprise; between the cafés shedding and the ones flat-out closing, it's bleak. You walk into a dive now, and it smells like potpourri or patchouli.
You can't smoke anywhere—not even on the terrace at ten below, where I'm alone. And when I'm on the sidewalk, there's always some joyless prick waving his arms dramatically to fend off my smoke, complaining about the smell.
Food-wise?
No more hot dogs drowning in béchamel and melted cheese.

The croque-monsieur went vegan.
The chef's salad became the garden salad.
The coffee machine spits soy lattes and sheep-milk matcha.
As for the scene,
Blue lighting has replaced the neon.
Pinball was swapped for poker machines and those horrible sports-betting terminals.
No jukebox anymore, but sometimes in the background, an impersonal lounge playlist from a streaming platform.
Otherwise, a brutal silence.
Teenagers and adults sitting alone, headphones on, in their own bubble. Isolated from the harsh reality.
Tables of one, with Wi-Fi and USB outlets everywhere, allowing them to react to "Reels" and posts. Communicating through keyboards and text messages. Connected through the filters of digital screens with FaceTime.
What a staggering irony.
In a world dominated by social networks, we have never been further away from each other.

It's no longer a place of tumult anymore; it's a rest area. A meditation room.
A terminus emptied of its meaning and its existence, and everything that once gave it its charm.
When we sat down, we were two, and we ended up being twelve.
We made friends; they collect virtual ones

We loaded our lives there; they charge their phones.
We made memories by living the moment; they upload the content of other people's lives.

And then there's mourning, the grief when life is slipping away.
With the disappearance of the cafés, the heart of France stops beating. Without them, the country loses its marrow, its digestion, its language, and its spine. Its pulse.
When the curtain falls and never rises again, it's like an old man falling asleep in his chair and never waking up. No screams and no official tears.
Just a closed door and one silence too many.
An absence that smells like the end.
What happens to a town that loses its mornings, its confidences, its arguments, and its laughter?
It becomes a ghost town. Without roots or memory.
I promise you. It's boring. It sucks.
I've seen cemeteries with more life than this.

But even tired—exhausted and drained—we must fight. Because every café that closes is another piece of the country's soul being erased.
This small world of ours was the last barricade before fast food; meals were simple and cheap.
We have to hold on because giving up is forgetting that it was the last place you could walk into without style, money, or a role.
Where you didn't need to lie.

A place where nothing looked sacred, and yet everything was.
God, I miss it.

I couldn't talk about places soaked in emotion and history without stopping for a while here.
For those of my age, maybe this chapter is a time machine. It might even bring a tear.
For the others—if this means nothing to you, that's fine. You had to be there to understand.
We lived it.
If this makes me sound like an old fart, so be it.
I'll own it.
Speaking of sadness and tragedy, might as well go all the way.
Because in our medical exam, if we cover restaurants as a body, everything that goes in must come out.
Right?
Then, it's time to go below the waist.
So let's stop at the rectum.
Yes. The asshole.
That's where the shit goes through, right?
So, we can move on to fast food.
It should be interesting.

Fast food

By a strange coincidence, this is the eleventh chapter of the book.
Chapter Eleven. That means bankruptcy, doesn't it?
How convenient. How fitting.
Because what you're about to read isn't a critique of fast food; it is the balance sheet of the evolution of our food habits.
Assets: Convenience, speed, and sugar.
Liabilities: taste, memory, and common sense.
Result?
Bankrupt.
Not just in the U.S., but everywhere, including in France. The world is in a state of colossal culinary debt. So, let's assess the damage.
A small warning:
The accountant is a French chef living in the US. That's going to be tricky.

A couple of years ago, we were on vacation in France. The weather was terrible that day, so I took my kids to see a movie. On our way, I suggested grabbing a bite beforehand. But as soon as the words left my mouth, I knew I'd fucked up. I thought, "Who is going to pick the restaurant?" I realized immediately that I had walked into a total SNAFU.
To escape this minefield, I organized a tactical retreat. And to avoid the same fate as Napoleon's

troops in Russia, I told my kids they could pick the spot.
Guess where I ended up?

I won't be a hypocrite; I won't say I never ate there. Of course I did. When I was younger or broke. Before the movies, or on nights when I couldn't face the stove. And yes—after the kind of hangovers where you need something, anything, to soak it all up. I won't lie: it works.
But here's what happened, and maybe you can relate.
Have you ever liked something in your youth, then tried it again ten years later out of curiosity? Only to think:
"How the hell did I ever like this?"
That is where I've been for the last fifteen years. I have never gone back. It doesn't go down anymore. My taste buds changed. My references evolved.
But if there is one thing that stayed exactly the same... it's this.

So as I parked the car and headed toward this "famous establishment," it hit me:
From the outside, the sign looks like the entrance to a circus. And the mascot—that clown plastered across the front—is laughing.
As he should be.
Believe me, Ronald has every reason to laugh at us.

Once inside, the place felt like a prefab unit—thrown together yesterday, rushed, and barely finished.
And yet, it is the exact opposite. Everything is meticulously designed and engineered by brilliant, Machiavellian minds.
I stood in line with other parents who, like me, were wondering what the hell we were doing there. I ordered from pictures on a giant board, paid, and grabbed my "food"—served without cutlery—on a tray that would shame a truck stop.
I headed into a room that looked like an elementary school cafeteria; the chairs and tables were in aggressive colors. It smelled like frying oil, rubber, and bleach.
We sat down, and right there, next to the table, there was the trash can. Stuffed with cardboard boxes and greasy wrappers.
Quick observation while I've got you... this is the only place on earth where customers will willingly sit down next to the toilets or the trash chute. Just saying.
Then I picked up that round, soft, greasy, floppy thing. I looked at it... and that was the exact moment I started wondering if something wasn't seriously off.
I wondered how the French—the "Flying Frogs" who invented every modern cooking technique in existence—how did we let ourselves be convinced that swallowing frozen burgers and dunking fries into ketchup was a good idea?

Wait. Hold on. Don't answer yet.

Swallow your food and wipe your hands. I'll be fair, and you can even finish your meal if you want. Because maybe you're reading this over a double bacon cheeseburger and fries soaking in ketchup, while your artificial vanilla milkshake is melting away, lining up for dessert.
Or maybe you're in a real restaurant, and you ordered a burger because,
—ultimate betrayal—
You now find this "thing" on the menu of every bistro and café in the country.

So let's have a look at it.
A spongy bun with no crust, no bite.
A flattened ground-beef patty—drained of color, temperature, flavor, and origin.
An industrial, neon-fluorescent sauce packed with sugar, smothering everything to hide the blandness.
And last but not least, orange, gelatinous squares branded as "cheese."
Seriously? In cheese country?
All of this is sold and served in a "restaurant" without a single cook or waiter.
Hold on a second. So, who made my... lunch?
An operator.
Someone who took pre-made components, pushed a button, and assembled this like a Lego.
That's it. Thanks. Bon appétit.
Come again?
Bon, what?
Is it just me? Am I the only one bothered by this?

Sure, let's set aside the one positive thing: anyone can do it, so it creates jobs.
But... we're talking about food here! Food you eat! It's like going to a hairdresser, and the guy behind you with the scissors is a plumber. Or leaving your car with a carpenter for maintenance.
For fuck's sake.

That reminds me: I once knew a guy who owned several fast-food franchises. I was curious how he responded when people asked what he did for a living.
Businessman.
Merchant.
Restaurant owner?
Don't laugh. That is exactly what he told me during a dinner. I nearly choked on my food and fell off my chair. What followed, of course, was an acrimonious argument about selling prepackaged items that go from a microwave to a fryer. He doesn't write his menu, and there is no craft.

I don't have a problem with the people who eat it; I have a problem with the ones who sell it.
It is food deception.
These brands sell you sugar-loaded, additive-packed products disguised as "simple, quick, and convenient."
Burgers are churned out on an assembly line, and ketchup is dripping everywhere.
Junk food is packaged and sold as a lifestyle with a subtitle that should just say:
Obscenity and obesity.

Those are the values of this new republic.
That's democracy by the stomach 2.0
That's cute.
Oh wait, I am not done. Let me tell you about my favorite part.
You can be in New York, Tokyo, London, Paris, or Lagos—the restaurants and the food are identical.
Same photos.
Same recipes.
Same ingredients.
Same names.
Same packaging.
The exact same standardized bite and the exact same cloned food. The same shit for everyone.
The only things that change are the language and the additives, depending on what's banned or allowed in each country.
Basically, you're poisoned according to your ZIP code.
And they have the nerve to push the envelope into this travesty of transparency. They print calorie counts like they're amendments to the Constitution for the... I was going to say "dishes"... How do you even call this stuff?
Guys, I don't know who's counting, but you need glasses and new batteries in your calculator. Or the other way around.
Wait, it's a combo, so perfidy is included.
Let's wrap it all up in a flashy box and toss in a plastic toy—a little figurine with as many chemicals as the food you're about to swallow.
And everybody will be happy.
You know what? Let's call it a "Happy Meal."

I never understood that in the US, anyone could be comfortable having forty percent of the American adult population being overweight. Among teenagers, it's twenty-three.
According to the CDC, in less than a decade, nearly two-thirds of adults in this country will be classified as obese.
Don't worry, folks, we are right behind you. Because the new generation in Europe is following the same path.
I'm not even talking about diabetes, allergies, or cancers caused by the chemicals used as seasoning.
It's pretty ironic that in France, we no longer advertise cigarettes or alcohol.
But these sugared, processed poisons?
No problem.
That's progress, apparently.

I consider myself lucky. Because of my age—and my job—I am one of those people who loves a product with a story, a season. I learned to appreciate what's cooked in a pan or an oven. I'm for meat with a name, bread that crackles, and sauce that takes time.
I grew up in kitchens that smelled of simmering pleasure, not melting plastic.
So yes, whenever I can, I fight back—Eye of the Tiger style. When my kids are hungry, I try to break the myth.
A snack? Bread and cheese.

A sandwich? A slice of pâté and gherkins, embraced by a crusty baguette.
A quick, cheap meal? A pack of pasta, cheese, and ham. Or an omelet.
At worst, a can of something. The difference? A can has an expiration date.
Your burger? Stick it in the fridge for six months, and it won't budge. In fact, after a while, it might actually come back to life. I'm not sure that's what people had in mind when they mentioned reincarnation.
For me, the real choice is in a restaurant. It's at the market, the grocery store, and in your own kitchen.
It is certainly not on a picture menu.
Most of the time, my kids look at me like I'm a boring, cranky old-timer. But every now and then, it works. They go:
"Yeah... that actually sounds pretty good."
With the phone in hand, the Uber Eats app open, and a finger already hovering over the last XXL combo from the nearest chain—drool already at the corner of their lip.
Smiling.
Brats.

But it's fine. I keep smiling, too.
Because I remember a time when Sundays meant eating with family or friends.
The menu?
A platter of cured meats. Roasted chicken and potatoes in the juice. Frisée salad with garlic. A

board of regional cheeses and a dessert from the pastry shop.
Leaving the table at four p.m.—stuffed and a bit intoxicated—after memorable conversations and acrimonious arguments. We reshaped the world according to our whims, our rants, and our laughter.
If today, people prefer to eat reconstructed chicken—fully aware of what they are eating—what do you want me to say?
Everyone does what they want. If it helps them keep the peace.
Well. Almost.
Because while you're on your phone or your iPad, you're being fed ads for frozen pizzas and ready-to-cook meals. Just in case you had no idea what to eat tonight.

I won't lecture or patronize, because we're all responsible. I'm not innocent either; I've got my share of skeletons. Even if I don't eat burgers, I buy junk at the supermarket like everybody else. We all have our bad tastes and guilty pleasures.
To be perfectly honest, as I'm writing this chapter, I am eating fried chicken drumsticks, hash browns, and spicy barbecue-garlic sauce.
Oh, shut the fuck up.
At least I made it all from scratch—even the sauce. And the fries are fresh.
I cooked it, so I am not a complete hypocrite.
Forgive me, people, for I have sinned. I had a craving.
Yes, I know—it looks bad. I admit it.

To hell with it.
Back to business.

Let's at least agree: there is a heavy hint of cynicism behind how they push these products.
By targeting tight budgets.
Well, the system understood early on that by making this food cheaper, louder, and more playful than anything else, it would win—not just the battle, but the war.
No money? Take the student menu, "buy one, get one free."

I'm not sure the issue is only about money. It's more nuanced than that.
First, let's blame it on our impatience and our laziness, sometimes physical, often intellectual.
Yes, spoiler alert: to cook, you have to drop the phone, get off the couch, and take the time.
Yes, I know it's challenging.
What annoys me is hearing people complain that eating properly is too expensive or too complicated.
Not necessarily.
You can eat well by eating simply—and affordably.
But if you want flavorful products that are cheap and available all year long, then don't be surprised when the food is bland and mediocre.
The problem is that by always wanting "cheaper," we got used to "less."
Last but not least, restaurants didn't become average for fun.

They adapted to our lowering standards.
To our obsession with price.
Junk food sells because some of us have forgotten the pleasure of cooking.
And if fast food wins, it's not because it's good.
It's because it's practical, easy, and predictable.
Cheaper than what's simple to make.
We made taste into a luxury.
Sad times.

The moral of the story is that the Three Musketeers, once protectors of French values, are no longer indomitable. Their cultural allegiance has shifted into a reverence for sugar.
Their moral compass has been disrupted by double-deckers.
As they surrendered, they traded their swords for plastic straws.
Wait, there's a problem; I only counted two.
I forgot; the third said he'd be late for the photo op at the Louvre with the French president.
He's at the drive-thru down the street, swallowing his honor between two sesame buns.
He hesitated—they also had panache in nuggets.
Tonight, both were on the menu.

Alright, alright. Let's get back on track.
After all this, my morale needs a boost—I am at rock bottom after writing this piece.
What if we went back to a real restaurant?
With fresh ingredients? And real cooks?
Let's take a look at the menu.

Wait. Not just yet.
Because when it comes to fast food, I don't have the same indulgence for the French as I do for the Americans.

Eating on Borrowed Time

I'll admit I might have been a bit harsh in the previous chapter, but I won't apologize. It bothers me to see people in France rushing into those places because I don't fucking get it.
In our country, meals have always been a structure. Anchors.
Reference points around which the day is organized.
Because the time spent at the table is sacred. We don't explain it or theorize it; it's like that, and everyone knows it. There's this unspoken agreement, that three times a day,
We sit down.
We order.
We wait.
We eat.
And we don't mess with that, because for us, it is the absolute rule of civility.

When I arrived in this country, I was struck by the contrast between the two continents when it comes to food and meals. it's a different culture
Not better. Not worse.
Just another way of living.
But not ours.
Fast food and takeout are not seen the same way; they serve a purpose.
They exist for a reason, and they make sense.
And it's no accident.
They match the rhythm.

Let’s start with breakfast, which was my first shock, my first cultural slap in the face.

For us, it is sacred, and according to the cliché, it's baguette, butter, jam, a croissant, or a pain au chocolat (what you call a chocolate croissant). It's not too sweet. But nothing salty. And as surprising as it seems, it’s the only meal we don’t cook.
Here it’s the exact opposite.
People wake up long before sunrise because school and work start early.
In the morning, some take the time to cook for themselves or for a family that’s still half asleep.
But as the days are long and brutal, breakfast is designed to stick to the stomach and to hold the line.
Eggs cooked in oil and bacon fried until the animal itself has been forgotten.
Bagels as thick as concrete blocks with cream cheese,
And when sugar shows up, it’s not for pleasure.
It’s strategic.
Pancakes drowned in an ocean of maple syrup.
Cereal served in bowls the size of a motorcycle helmet, with half a liter of milk or peanut butter and jelly sandwiches.
By the way, one of the things that you eat leaves us speechless. Peanut butter! We don’t just get it.

But for others, that is even too slow.

So at six-thirty in the morning, while I'm trying to gather my mental faculties and struggling to remember my own name, half the country is already in their cars, pedal to the floor. As if they were afraid the day might start without them. Trying to catch up and already looking behind schedule before they've even begun anything. After working here for a while, I understood why. Because, precisely, the first stress of the day is being late. It's a red flag.
In every company, every profession, you clock in. On a terminal, a computer, or an old-school punch clock. And it is neither understanding nor forgiving.
So since you don't have time to sit down, in order to satisfy the hunger, which isn't productive, it's a waste of time. You grab the first meal of the day on the way, wherever the car stops. Gas stations. Drive-through. Coffee shops. Some place glowing like a lighthouse at the corner of an intersection. It's not a destination. It's a pit stop. You refuel and move on.
And everything is ordered to go.
Coffee in a cup that smells stronger than it tastes, sealed with a lid; god forbid if you spill it, I might slow you down.
Food locked inside Styrofoam boxes.
It's not eaten. It's swallowed in the car. One hand on the wheel, the other in a paper bag. It rides shotgun in the passenger seat
You eat while driving, stuck in traffic, on the phone prepping meetings, reading yesterday's

report, or finishing the last touches on the make-up.
Breakfast happens in motion; it doesn't interrupt the morning.
It isn't a ceremony; it's preparation.
It isn't sacred; it's practical.
You can eat half-asleep, walking, standing, sitting on the edge of the bed, or on your way to wherever you need to go.
As long as the stomach is full and the brain has fuel, thinking starts, and you can function.
Therefore, produce.
You have no time for this bullshit at this hour because the day is already waiting.
That's breakfast in America.

Regarding lunch, there are two ways to handle it.
Ours
Believe it or not, it's a law. We are so obsessed with meals and food that lunch breaks are legally protected. And to be honest, eating at your desk is frowned upon.
Yours,
At noon, nothing really stops either.
Not for anybody, even me—it's usually the time in the kitchen when I get carpet bombed by takeout tickets.
But from where I stand, your lunch is called a break. But it rarely feels like one. It's an optimistic intermission, just a parenthesis between meetings, emails, and deadlines.
Some reheat leftovers and eat with their eyes already glued to their computer screens, phone in

hand. But most of the time, when food shows up, it's in the shape of a sandwich.
Stratified
Layered.
The bread wraps the filling. Paper neutralizes and secures everything.
The bag carries those layers between you and hunger. Insulating desire from regret and pleasure from duty. And you eat standing up, at your desk, or in the car with the engine running and the AC blasting.
It patches things up, like duct tape on a cracked pipe.
You eat to hold on. What matters is not collapsing at three p.m.
Lunch doesn't interrupt the day either; it supports it—like a brace on a bad knee.
Because once again, the clock doesn't stop.

Another difference.
We don't nibble outside of meals.
We don't stuff ourselves with snacks all day long because hunger is part of the ritual. And it's not socially well-perceived.
Except, of course, for the two daily aperitifs, which are non-negotiable.
Yes, there are two: one before lunch and one before dinner. And if you do only one, I'll tell you right now, that's sacrilege.

Here, and all day long, I see people snack. As if you don't want to feel hunger. Oversized protein

bars and supposedly healthy snacks packed with sugar. Chemical energy drinks.
Fourteen-syllable iced coffees and teas, torn between glucose syrup and chemically added sugar. Even though you were told they contain zero calories. Food corporations that make those things lie all day long about the food, like politicians delivering campaign promises.

Then comes dinnertime.
Once again, early. Always too early for my appetite.
I remember one of my first invitations from friends.
I was asked to come over around six. I thought, well, it's perfect, right on time for a glass of wine and some finger food to stimulate the appetite.
Wrong.
Five minutes after I arrived, dinner was on the table.
You should have seen my face when they asked me to sit down.

From whom I've heard or noticed, outside of social or professional gatherings, families don't always eat together on a regular basis anymore.
It's mostly when they can.
Otherwise, it's a rolling service. Everyone eats when they want, and not necessarily the same thing.
The first time I saw it, I told myself

"Well, it's like a restaurant. Open bar, open kitchen—but at what time does the cleaning crew come in?"

Food is cooked quickly, often something you know by heart. Something simple that doesn't ask questions. Served before hunger really settles in. People eat alone. Standing at the counter. On the couch. Plate on their knees. In front of a football game.
I get it.
People come home wrecked, crushed by pressure. The day stuck to their body like a bad hangover. Dinner isn't a celebration and doesn't linger. It doesn't pretend to be memorable; it repairs before the day drains you completely.
Most of the time, that's enough.

On weekends, it's different.
Dinner is ordered.
It arrives in brown paper bags and is usually fried. Boxes are stacked on the table; everyone chooses their comfort food.
Portions are generous, and leftovers are expected. People reunite briefly, often out of family politeness. Kids talk about school.
Then pretty quickly, everyone pulls out their phone.
The TV hums like a third adult in the room, already advertising tomorrow's menu.

So why are we so different?

In France, most of the time meals stop the day. Because hunger is often emotional, we eat because it's time and because the table is set. Sitting down means spending time together, arguing and laughing, and socializing.
Even if we don't have the same relationship to food, meals, and the table, I don't think it's a question of taste. That would give it too much credit.
Nor is it culture in the romantic sense.
It's a question of time.
One culture built meals around moments where work fades and life takes over. Food fills the space that sharing time creates.
The other one built meals to follow you and negotiate with the clock. Sometimes politely, most of the time under stress. They fill the space-time leaves.
Neither is wrong.
They respond to different lives, different pressures, and different urgencies.
In the United States, meals were designed so the day doesn't buckle and, above all, so it never slows down. Time bends around the table, not the other way around, because somehow a table ends up being just a surface, a piece of furniture. So people share space and calories, but never the moment.
Eating is a function. And food is like an item or a line on your schedule. It is held in the hand and sits in the car, and it fits in your agenda.
Like some temporary fuel to stay upright.
You don't overthink it.

You don't analyze it.
You don't somatize.
No poetry. No ritual. No romanticism

After twenty years, I don't judge anymore.
But my body still does. I feel it in my rhythm.
But I categorically refuse to sign that contract. I still instinctively wait for food to stop the world, even for a short moment. Even when it has no intention of doing so. Not like food here, which always has somewhere to go. By bike, scooter, or car.
That's why it's sometimes hard for French people to adapt here.
Some manage.
Some endure.
And others linger but never change the way they eat.
Like me.
I'm one of those who grit their teeth.
I am one of those who still prefer eating with cutlery rather than holding food in my hands.
Even if in my job we rarely have time to sit down.
So we eat standing in a corner or while walking or doing something else.
Like you.
See, we're not that different after all.

In the end, this country mirrors today's world.
Always on the move, always something to do.
Everything is in motion.
And it irritates me.

Because I know trends always come from the west, and this model spreads everywhere. Food circulates, arteries clog like traffic, but the system keeps going.
There's a certain irony in eating nonstop in a society obsessed with never stopping.
Like this chapter that won't end.
Had enough?
Good.
Now you know how I feel.

One last thing.
I miss Paris;
I miss the natural nonchalance of the French way of life.
But what scrambles my eggs is, as I'm a masochist and a psycho, I miss New York too.
And Manhattan is the purest expression of that speed.
Let's admit it.
Duality has its charm.
So does my schizophrenia.

Clichés and bad habits die hard

"But you're French." Lovely.
AWESOME.
AHHH, Parisss.
Yes, that's what I hear twenty times a day, for the past twenty years.
And I very much learned something important, which I have shared with my countrymen who arrive in this country.
When you meet someone here, don't get cocky and think France is the center of the world. It might be yours, but you'll be slapped back to reality pretty quickly.
So, if someone asks you where you're from, you have to be precise. Don't casually say you're from Paris, just like that, out of the fucking blue.
Because most of the time they'll think Paris... Texas.
I reassure you, not for long. After hearing a few words from you with that cringy accent. You won't be able to fool anybody.
My advice is, it's better to start by saying you're French and only then drop the city.
By the way, I was surprised by the number of cities bearing the names of actual towns in France: Versailles, Montpellier, and so on.
In Miami, there's even an entire neighborhood where all the streets have French names: Bourgogne Street, Normandie Street, etc.

I like to think that Americans do like the French.

To a certain point.
You are fond of our food. You like the French culture, the style, and the elegance.
But this is where it stops.
I've witnessed several times that once the enchantment fades, there's always a smile—no, Let's be precise, a grin—that appears on your interlocutor's face. Like mild discomfort or a slight embarrassment.
As if you were saying:
"Well... it's okay. Nobody's perfect."
Admit it, you can be slightly condescending toward us sometimes, almost asking whether we have electricity or running water in France.
And I know that our manners and our quirks get on your nerves. Trust me, I get it. I am French, and even I sometimes get annoyed by it.
I could add that the fact that so few of us are able to say two lines in English still puzzles your mind.
Honestly, you're not entirely wrong.
When it comes to foreign languages, we suck.
It's not in our DNA.
I've got friends who've lived here for fifteen years, and when you hear them speak, you'd swear they landed yesterday.
Me? I don't have the stereotypical French accent. Never have. In some sentences or words, you will detect that I am not from here.
To my surprise, most of the time, people think I'm Canadian. Which is mildly awkward and worries me.
To you, they are distant cousins. Slightly dumb and endlessly mockable, right?

Don’t be shocked; we have the same; we have the Belgians.
Not very nice—for Belgians, and even less for Canadians.
Alright. Let’s even things out.
You know what people say:
The reason the French love Belgian jokes so much is because they’re easy to understand—even for us.
There.

Anyway, since I have been there, the adjustment has been easy enough—the country is welcoming. Life here is a bit tougher. Way more expensive. Much faster. And more ruthless than in Europe. Which makes sense. That’s the system: sink or swim. But I like it.
What was harder to swallow was Miami.
A city—I've hated this city since day one.
At least I’m consistent.
I won’t redo the eulogy of that shithole—it’s in the previous book. And I will not pretend to be polite and feed you bullshit. Anybody who knows me can tell you straight: no, I don’t like living here.
I just can’t stand it.
I'd rather take any city in the US but here. But to go where? To be perfectly honest, my blood boils in Paris and New York.

Where was I?
Ah yes,
As for you Americans, you’re very approachable, cordial, polite, and generally pleasant.

You're warm, sure, partly because you get on a first-name basis fast. English helps with that. No formal/informal split between "you and you."
So you get comfortable quickly.
You speak loudly and reassure a lot.
It's convenient.

Even if I've been here long enough for the initial shock to fade, I've never fully gotten used to your eating habits. There are still plenty of things I haven't digested or simply refuse to swallow.
It's little things, details, and yet, sometimes, I still don't fully understand what's going on.
Maybe that's where the real difference begins to show.
Food.

No Kitchen Required.

I know I told you why I granted you some clemency about fast foods, but don't be greedy, and don't get too comfortable;
Because let's see what happens when we all stop running and you and I meet in the supermarket.
Well, I'm faced with a whole new set of headaches.
First, what's hard for me is I've lost my comfort food; French brands are getting rarer in Miami, so it's hard to find my childhood cookies and all the shitty treats I swallow in a hurry, hidden in a closet—to avoid that I-feel-sorry-for-your-ass look on my boss's face. My wife
Yogurts. Don't even think about it. Here it's too gelatinous, offensively sweet, or chemically sweetened to death for me.
Vegetables? Radishes, celeriac, artichokes, fennel, endives... not exactly popular here, more like exotic curiosities.
I can't even count how many times I showed up at the checkout with my vegetables and the cashier looks at me in a weird way, wondering, "Dude, "You really eat those things? I thought it was a plant, some decoration?"
One day I found rhubarb. I was in a hurry to go home to make a tart, but when I paid, the cashier asked me, "What the fuck is that?"
The other day I even had one ask me what an olive tasted like, because she'd never eaten one.
What do you want me to say?

I said, “It tastes like olive.”
Judging by her face, she didn’t appreciate my answer. Once again, I passed for a rude asshole—like a proper Frenchman.
No big deal. I’m used to it.

Cheese is another problem.
Nothing that smells or runs away. Hard and gelatinous cheeses. Mozzarella sticks, cheddar, and ultra-pasteurized, plasticized camembert, which you call brie here.
I can’t. Sorry. Too French for that.
By the way, I know that “camembert” is a bitch to say, so you renamed it. I don’t blame you. But it’s not the same region, and it’s not the same cheese; Camembert is from Normandy, and brie is from the suburbs of Paris. Just saying.
The New York cheesecake doesn’t come from Tucson, right?
French wine? Five or six varieties in the store, not more.
All American products are adapted to your taste, and that’s normal. After all, you’re home, goddamned.
So I know what you're going to say: shut the fuck up or go back to where you come from.
Don’t misunderstand me; I love your country.
But I have to complain.
I don’t want to lose my citizenship.
There are some requirements to remain French.
It's written in small lines at the bottom of the passport.

Now, let's tackle another matter...
In France, we cook every night and especially for Sunday lunch. Otherwise, weekends, whether Friday or Saturday are usually the evenings we go to a restaurant
Here I am surprised to see that three-quarters of what is in the carts in the supermarket is already pre-cooked food, whether frozen or vacuum sealed.
So when do you guys cook?
Don't tell me weekends; I won't buy it. You order ready-to-eat and get it delivered.
And as a chef, it worries me.
Because in the end, what gets transmitted?
The taste for instant gratification.
The reflex of using an app and the convenience of clicking a button.
We're no longer passing down taste, or a gesture, or a "savoir-faire." Just the art of complaining when you burn yourself opening the container or whining when it arrives cold.

Now, I'm going to tell you a secret, but you can't repeat it. I am going to be in trouble with my fellow countrymen. And they will call me a fucking hypocrite.
Because you sold it to me too—the French bumpkin. I am like you now. I am in.
On three sacred days of the week, Sunday and Monday, I behave like the regular American.
You know what I am getting at, right?
I watch football and eat finger food.

And worse, on Thursday night at work, I have the game playing on the phone, sitting in the window during the service.
The only thing is, even though I've always loved the sport, at every commercial break, I have to get up and get away from the TV or the screen.
Watching all those ads for brands pushing burgers dripping with saturated fat and shining like sex objects is torture for me.
Somehow food isn't desired anymore—it is imposed. Always available, one app away.
Ready to be consumed without a second thought.
Portions are obscene, and there's no middle ground.
Excess passes for generosity.
Restraint for anti-Americanism.
Between the two—nothing. No balance.
The problem is, the second I reach the kitchen, there's a beer commercial.
Now I'm thirsty.
So, when I plant myself back on the couch, I have a cold brew in my hand.
Hats off; you are fucking geniuses.

And during all this time, I watched friends, family, and—I am guessing most of you—wolf down stuff I wouldn't feed my dog.
Yes—Rocky. My golden retriever.
Remember him?
There is a whole chapter about him in the first book. Yes, I know it's weird, but I love the goofball.

Though honestly, I am sure that furry glutton would probably dive into it like a starving beast.
How do I know?
Because my kids eat like you, and the second the food gets delivered, the dog sniffs it, slides under the table ninja-style, and drools.
Ready to clean up the floor if anything falls.
He figured out the system.
Smart dog.
Makes sense.
He's American.

Maybe this whole thing isn't about buns versus baguettes.
Maybe it's about logistics.
In the United States, delivery isn't a treat.
It's infrastructure. It's as normal as electricity.
Food circulates like blood in an optimized body.
On bikes. In cars. In thermal bags big enough to smuggle a small nation.
Nearly sixty percent of the food budget is spent outside the home.
Which means the kitchen is optional.
It became a nostalgic concept, like handwriting.
In France, delivery exists too.
But mostly at night or on weekends.
After a long day. Or after too much wine and not enough planning.
It's backup. Not a backbone.
Only about a third of food spending happens outside the home, which is mostly in restaurants.
Groceries still win.

The stove still matters, and wait to see what's coming to you if you forget the butter or the cheese when you come from the groceries. That's not romance or superiority.
That's architecture.

In America, ultra-processed food isn't an exception. It's structural.
Engineered. Distributed. Normalized.
In France, it's present, of course, but it still feels slightly suspicious. Like a polite guest who stays too long and rearranges your furniture.

So we face a battle between productivity and ritual.
And in the middle, me.
Outdated.
A helpless romantic with a fork in hand. Refusing to choose convenience over memory.
Debating with my kids why I should download the Uber Eats app and being yelled at because they need faster Wi-Fi.
I'm not even judging. I'm observing. I'm just watching how our relationship to food has become urbanized and marketed.
Before: a dish.
Today: a concept, a tribe, a claim.
It's not even food anymore—it's an identity, a posture.
People want to eat well and fast, without knowing what "cooking" actually means.
And that's where everything tips over.

Because today, we eat the idea of a product, not the product itself.
Inevitably, when you change the way you eat,
You change the way you cook.
And you change the way you live.
So what you eat at home slowly dictates what you expect when you go out.
Same reflexes.
The same food, just served on a plate, on a tablecloth, with a check at the end.
That's when the restaurant stops being a destination and becomes a continuation.
And when I'm not in the supermarket or in my own kitchen, I'm in your playground.
Cooking for you,
With that in mind.

Bullshit

We—cooks, chefs, and sous-chefs—are the product of an education, a memory, and a tradition we try to keep alive. And our work is, by definition, a tribute to the old days.
We are the guardians of the temple.
We work with products that have personality.
Some are rough, others delicate.
We prepare them, we season them, and they transform in contact with temperature and seasoning, but not with the world
They don't throw tantrums, they don't have moods, and they don't lie.
They don't bend to trends, contrary to clients, restaurant owners, and critics.
I could even add the staff to the list.
So this chapter is not specifically about food but about all the bullshit we piled on top of it.
The foam. The morality. The panic.

In my kitchen, every time I read tickets, I know that things have changed. But it happened slowly, order after order.
And now meals have a very specific taste, that modern mix of "good intentions" on display... and very real control underneath.
So first, we had to accept that some dishes disappeared from restaurant menus.
Especially here in Miami.

I'll set aside snails and onion soup, which somehow still show up everywhere in French restaurants.
But I wondered for a while, why do certain dishes fall into oblivion?
Well, Because they've become harder to sell. Because we don't share the same culinary culture, and customers don't have those dishes as references. And when there's no reference, the desire to eat them evaporates—because there's no memory attached.
It's that simple.

And the cherry on top: we have to swallow the dictatorship of appearances.
Because in our modernized world, you photograph what you eat, and chefs do the same for the meals they put on the menu on social media.
And this where it all go weird
Because a calf's brain doesn't play well on a post. It screams Roman orgy.
Explaining what sweetbread is terrifies some lighthearted souls raised on avocado toast and ground beef.
A pig's foot is too real for a generation raised on reconstructed chicken—skinless, tasteless, and above all, historyless.
Veal kidneys and livers look too "animal." And if you order it, people look at you like you're related to Hannibal Lecter
It's striking, in our time, how thin the line has become between cannibalism and carnivores

Anything that reminds us of what was once alive must be erased.
These days, anything that resembles an animal, or the second there's a drop of blood, is forbidden in the name of decency.
Everything people eat now has to be boneless.
Sliced ham, but not on the bone
A ribeye, but not a T-bone
So customers eat only chicken breasts, tenderloins, and overcooked meat.
As for fish, it must be filleted.
Don't you dare send out a whole fish and leave the head on, even for a shrimp. Or you've got a diplomatic incident on your hands.
In short, everything gets deboned—except stupidity.
It needs to be safe. Infantilized, sanitized...
Let's take oysters, for example. You shuck them, cut the foot, soak them in water, and put them back in the shell.
What the fuck?
Let me tell you that the first time I saw that, I went into the walk-in and cried.
Alone, desperate, heartbroken.

In France, when I was a kid and went to the butcher, I had a photo of the cow my chateaubriand came from.
Well, in Miami there are no butchers, so the problem solves itself.

But try doing that in a restaurant or a supermarket—you're socially exiled. Cancelled. We've forgotten that food comes from the soil, the garden, the farm, the cheesemonger, the butcher, and the fishmonger.
Today, it comes from marketing. You buy meat, toilet paper, fish, and dish soap in the same place. It's neutral. Convenient. Frictionless.
In supermarkets, grocery shopping has become a conversation between packaging and consumer—between the product and the person who's about to shove it into the microwave.
Marketing replaced taste.
Seasonality is over.
Sure, there are no market gardeners here, and no real seasons either, so that doesn't help.
But for fuck's sake—strawberries in winter, tomatoes in February.
Here's a fun one: ask a youngster when peaches grow. I bet they'll answer:
"All year, right?"
Blissfully Ignorant

So food has to be smooth, reassuring, and non-threatening.
Not shocking.
No edge.
And preferably sauce on the side.
S.O.S., as we call it in a kitchen.
Funny thing, it means "mayday" in French.
See, you've been warned.

Something you can swallow without thinking.
Without emotion.
But when cooking disappears, taste becomes theoretical.
And when taste becomes theoretical,
You bring your shortcuts with you.
Your impatience.
Your fear of waiting.
Your need for speed.
And then you sit at my table, and you expect the same reflexes, just plated.On a white tablecloth
That's when I realize
I'm not only cooking food.
I'm cooking against habit.

If supermarkets are the good mirror of a society ... Restaurants are the perfect mirror of a generation —with its rituals, its people, its trends, and its contradictions. And its mind games.
That's why we, behind our stoves, see all this coming like a tsunami. And even if we try to hold the line, the dam is leaking. So we retreat into our kitchens and stay among ourselves. Pan neurotics. Cooking-time neuropaths. Sauce psychotics. And we comfort ourselves with our motherland food, wherever we go.
Because what escapes us—those of us who live for and through cooking—isn't technique.
It's people.
And since we're about as comfortable with people as a vegan is with a meat cleaver, the dining room is a galaxy far, far away to us.
Never forget this line from Anthony Bourdain:

“Why are all chefs drunks?
Because we don’t understand why the world
doesn’t work like our kitchens.”

The menu

Alright. Now that you have a better idea of what's going on, let's go back inside a restaurant. I am going to give you a chef coat, and we are going to spend some time together.

We've talked about places, time, food, and the question of choice. But there's one fundamental subject nobody ever talks about.

And you—laymen, pilgrims, or simple food lovers —You who sit down at a table and order a dish without thinking too much about it—

Have you ever wondered how that damn menu is made?

How did that thing come to life?

Do we just wing it?

Or is there something else going on?

What's really behind it?

Well, this entire chapter is dedicated to the art of the menu.

Welcome to our private hell—where aspirin is our trophy.

Being a chef is, for me, the greatest job in the world, but it comes with a price; the job never stops. Because once you've nailed the recipe and the plating, you still have to phrase the dishes and sell them.

That's the internal mess of a restaurant. Not that it is brain surgery, but it matters.

And making a menu isn't just typing words on laminated paper—it's like a marriage.

You have to compromise.
But where it gets complicated, it's a threesome.
Yeah, "a ménage à trois."
It sounds sexy and promising, basically the French cliché fetishist. Right?
Wrong.
Meet the infernal trio.

The boss

It's his restaurant, his baby, so he wants his ideas, his obsessions, and his grandmother's recipe.
Completely normal—that's his restaurant.
So far, so good.
Then one day he comes to you with a recipe his other half made the night before, and he wants to put it on the menu to please her. Because she complains he never listens to her.
So you make it, you hate it, and you shut the fuck up, even if it's bland or the recipe tastes like shit.
You don't agree?
Well, it's your kitchen; you could say something.
You're the chef, after all.
Yeah, sure.
Go explain to the guy who signs your paycheck that his wife cooks like a potato.
Been there, true story.

The customers

Now this is where it gets tense.
It's the jungle.

You have to juggle the neighborhood mood,
trends, invented intolerances, egos, whims, and
the arrogance of the local wildlife.
And there's a new thing:
Everyone is a chef now.
How many times have I heard customers say:
"I'm a chef, like you."
I go:
"Oh yeah? Where?"
The lady answers, dead serious, without blinking:
"At home."
Then you get the greatest hits
"At home, I do the same."
"If I were you, I'd put a bit more..."
"If I were you, I'd do it like this or like that."
I think that sentence—*"If I were you"*—is the one
I've heard the most in my career. And every time I
pinch myself not to be rude, but the words are
right there, burning my lips
"You know what? Open a restaurant, push one
hundred and fifty covers per service... and stop
busting my balls."

But to be fair, there's a twist.
Ironically, in a restaurant, I can send in a beurre
blanc in under three minutes.
A béarnaise in under four.
A hundred covers under forty-five minutes—no
problem.
Write a menu for a group of fifty-five? I'll do it
between an appetizer and a main.
But cook for four at home, and if my wife asks for
mayonnaise at the same time,

I'm fucking lost.
Which naturally brings us to the third member of the trio...

The chef

Now we're walking through a minefield because he's the most unstable of the three.
Susceptible, hot-headed, and not very objective.
And most of the times, if the recipe isn't his, he'll always find something wrong with it.
Not me talking. That's fifteen years in kitchens and thirty years living around chefs every day.
We have an ego big enough to feed an entire regiment.
But let me explain how we think.
We're stubborn and a bit capricious, so we want to write our menu our way, with our recipes. And if you don't like it, it's because you don't know anything or you don't understand shit. You're basically a Boeotian.
I'm not saying that in a negative or caricatural way. It's just a reflex. Because we're always convinced we have the right taste, the right dish, and the right seasoning.
And that's not always true.
The main quality of a chef is accepting he can be wrong. Not just "listening" to others' points of view, but actually taking them into account.

And here, regarding suggestions and opinions, we're spoiled.

because we have to deal with gluten-free, vegetarian, vegan, and lactose-free demands. Allergies, sensitivities, and... everyday bullshit.
I even know restaurants where the chef doesn't use pepper anymore, just to avoid trouble.
Because here comes the sauce served by the ladle
... Rolling drums...
The customer is king...
So, sometimes, after a long service, we are asked to make a dish to satisfy this joyful crowd, and it pisses us off.
Let me tell you, you put such bad will into making it that you end up proving to the owner it's too long, too complicated... and too expensive.
If any chef reads this and claims he's never done that, let him cast the first stone.
Oh—you can't find one?
Yeah, right.
Bullshit,

Alright. Once the compromises are made, two questions remain.
First.
Why do we put some dishes on a menu and not others?
If I were playful and it were my choice only, I'd put this on the menu.
Exactly like that to the last fucking dot.
It's self-explanatory and saves a lot of time and headaches.

STARTERS

—Escargots.
Garlic, butter, and I don't provide Tic Tacs.
—Country pâté, rillettes, and rosette de Lyon
Gherkins and onions are provided.
—Celeriac rémoulade.
Lots of mayo; lots of mustard. That's the point.
—Leeks and vinaigrette
Will make you pee.
—Herring with potatoes in oil
If you don't like onions, move on.
—Frisée, lardons, garlic croutons, and poached egg.
Frisée is a salad, not a haircut.
—Whelks, gray shrimp, with aioli.
The French kind: Potato, garlic, and real mayo
—Eggs and mayo.
Don't forget to check for bits of parsley between your teeth before going back to work.
—Fish soup, rouille, and garlic croutons
Yes, garlic again.
—Vol-au-vent
With a lot of béchamel, yes, there is flour, milk, and... garlic.
—Roasted bone marrow with truffle
Bread is mandatory.

MAINS

—Beef bourguignon.
At least six liters of red wine went into this.
—Veal blanquette.
Gluten, meat, butter, and milk—your worst nightmare. Cannot be made otherwise. Forget it.

—Ribeye and dauphinois gratin.
No cheese on the gratin, a rookie mistake, and béarnaise is unlimited.
—Roasted lamb leg & flageolets.
Will make you fart. And there is garlic.
—Endives Ham Gratin
You'd better be hungry. It's a little rich. Well, very rich.
—Roasted chicken & house mashed potatoes.
The boss forced me to. Out of spite, I added garlic.
—Steak tartare, hand-cut fries.
Raw. I will not cook it. Not happening. Drop it.
—Sole meunière.
Yes, the head is there; don't faint. it's deboned table-side, so everything will be alright
—Seafood platter.
If you like getting your hands dirty.
—Moules marinières.
Same thing, but with onion breath.
—Grilled sweetbreads.
Lots of butter. Dare if you have the courage.
— Veal kidneys with old-style mustard sauce.
Nobody will judge you.
—Pot-au-feu.
If you want to feel healthy.
—Cassoulet.
If you don't.
—Duck confit
Cooked in fat. Medium rare is not an option.

DESSERT

—Aged cheese plate.
Very aged. Stinky. Runny. Smelly. Red wine is not optional.
—Lemon meringue tart.
Could not find a joke.
—Pink praline tart
If you like orgasms.
—Floating island.
You might want to check your blood sugar before and after.
—Paris-Brest.
Hope you're in for butter and gluten.
—Profiteroles.
I'm not paying for your dry cleaning.
—Grand Marnier soufflé.
Takes time. You're allowed to scroll on Instagram while you wait.
—Chocolate mousse
Complain to the person who asked me to put the chicken on the menu.

Caustic, isn't it?
Looks good, right?
Hungry?
Well—you're going to starve, buddy, because it's impossible.
I'd be out of business in four months from food costs and staffing alone. And right before bankruptcy, I'd end up in jail for stabbing every customer who asked for modifications.
Not to mention I threw my team into the fryer because they couldn't keep up.

Second question.
How the hell do you organize this menu?
Let's look at the strategies and the twisted brains hiding behind them.

—The lazy ones.
Alphabetical order. That's it.
—The pragmatic ones.
By price, low to high or high to low. No poetry.
—The rebels.
They put whatever they want in whatever order they want. And if you don't like it, too bad.
—The sneaky ones.
By profit. They know you never read to the bottom, so the margins go on top, and the sweat goes on the bottom.
—The nerds.
Concept junkies. Excel sheets. Stats. PowerPoints. All that to decide where to place a fucking salad
—The hopeless romantics.
Like me.
We write a menu like we play a guitar solo. With flashes, wrong notes, hesitations, and moments of grace. A menu that breathes.

But there's another scenario.
Now, if the chef is also the owner, that's a different story.
On the menu, he'll rank dishes by emotion, not by price.
Look at the first four lines of each section—that's where his heart is. His ego. His pleasure.
Those ones he babies. He gives them everything.

The rest?
Important but not as much,
He will give them attention, not love.

That's how a menu is made.
How it lies. How it's born. How it survives.
And above all, how it keeps a place alive—through chaos, egos, compromises, strokes of genius, and exhaustion.
The bottom line is a menu is a love-hate story.
Moments of brilliance.
Crossed-out ideas.
Dishes you love.
Dishes you regret.
Dishes you keep just to "look good."
And in the worst case, some you can't stand.
It's a poem written in a minefield. Something wobbly, often honest, sometimes rigged, but always sincere.
It's a painting you keep redrawing. constantly, because the economic reality never leaves. It has to be profitable, follow the times, and somehow still carry a promise of pleasure.
Yes, like a book.
Speaking of which. I've realized that my menus sell way better than my books.
My boss is happier than my editor.
Shocking.
Well, I'll take it.
Thanks for the vote of confidence.

Now that you know what's behind each line, the next time you open a menu, give it the respect it deserves.
It survived a civil war and nuclear-level arguments.

But wait—it's not over.
Now that you've got the bird, it still has to fly on its own.
Because across from me—whether customers or servers—I'm dealing with a whole new breed of species. Fueled by matcha, soy milk, and grilled tofu in avocado oil.
And me?
I'm French. I'm fifty-three. And I'm old school.
So if I want to survive in this new world, I have to understand it—and adapt.
And there... That's really not a given.
Damn, all this has opened my appetite. I am starving; I'm going to take a break and make something to eat, and I need a glass of wine.

Collateral Damage

So what do we do with all this mess?
With all these culinary and cultural upheavals, with these new trends and fashions coming from God knows where.
How do you adapt in restaurants to please all these people and to stay relevant when you're a French chef in Miami?
I know—I told you this wasn't a chef's book.
Sorry. I can't help myself.

Well, you make modern menus. Simple.
Accessible. Low-risk.
So what's left:
—Salmon tartare
The universal starter that offends no one.
—Chicken.
As easy to sell as a sheet of printer paper.
—A salmon fillet.
Often farmed, therefore tasteless; same logic as the starter.
—A tuna steak.
As long as there's any left... But if you think you're selling it tataki style (seared but raw), you're dreaming. And I'll still have to explain to someone that a steak isn't necessarily beef.
—A burger
No choice.
—A bowl
Oh yeah, they love that—it speaks to their chakras.

—A risotto made with vegetable stock and no parmesan.
—Vegetable pasta, or if you're feeling confident and lucky, go for a ragù sauce.
But don't even think about beef tartare.
Nobody will try it; nobody will sell it.
One day a server saw me swallow raw meat. Since then, he looks at me in a weird way. And when I get close to him, he gets nervous.

Let's not kid ourselves, because I want to defend them; they are collateral victims as well.
It's not just us cooks suffering from these tectonic shifts. Servers are taking it too.
They suffer because they're like us, except they're on the front line, in the light, talking to people.
I have immense respect for them.
But let's be honest, there are several species.
Like in wildlife documentaries.

There's the Server 2.0:

— Tattooed from the right ankle to the cartilage of the left ear. Alright. It's a look.
— No notepad, "because I remember everything." We'll see about that.
— He speaks the same language as the customers. Great. So far, so good.
— He's vegan. That doesn't bother me, but since he refuses to taste anything, he doesn't know the menu. On top of that, he's in a phase of a no-gluten diet, and he doesn't like pepper.

So how do you sell your dishes, buddy, if you don't even know what they taste like?
If you don't taste, you don't learn.
If you don't learn, you don't know shit.
And you make a fool of yourself.

Here's an example.
One day I'm serving scallops as the special, and I show them to the head waiters.
One of them tells me:
— No, I don't eat that; I don't like fish.
Alright. It's not fish, but let's move on. Let's not get picky.
Another one tries it, eats a bite, and then says,
— It tastes funky, and the texture is weird; it looks almost like a chicken fucked a fish.
I look at him, surprised and slightly irritated, and I say,
— It's a shellfish. It's seafood.
True story. I swear.

Alright, for fun—another one.
One day I make a salad with crab "meat."
That detail matters; you'll see why.
At the beginning of service, a server comes up to me. But I will let you enjoy the dialogue.
Him: "Chef, how much should I charge for the 'meat salad,' and what doneness should I suggest?"
Me: "The crab is cooked in water but served cold."
He hesitates. Then, with a disgusted face, he goes:
"A salad with boiled cold meat?"
Me: "No, it's crab."

Him: “But you told me it was meat.”
I stare at him and then give him a moment to see if something happens.
He stopped at the word 'meat,' trying to figure out which animal it was. And as nothing seemed to ring a bell, to end his suffering, and mostly mine, I’m forced to add
— It’s crab flesh. The thing with claws.
Him: Ahhhhhh, okay, so it’s a fish salad.
Now the surprise switches sides, and I just look at him.
You know what? I gave up.
Go figure.
Again, it's a true story. You can’t make this up; sometimes reality is funnier than fiction.

And my favorite: the one who truly doesn’t give a damn.
Customer asks:
— “What’s the fish of the day?”
Answer:
— “Uh... I don’t know; I’ll ask the kitchen.”
Come on, man. You work here. You could ask before going on the floor. A server who doesn’t know the menu is like a cop who doesn’t know how to use his gun.

Sadly, this is our everyday life, because this job is becoming a paycheck occupational hazard. A way to pay bills. Some of them are in restaurants while waiting for something else:
the TikTok revelation, a DJ career, a Netflix casting, an imaginary start-up, or a spiritual road

trip. Working in a restaurant is not a career for them anymore; it's a transit zone.
So they vanish on break every twenty minutes to drink maté between two tables.
They get offended by anything.
And sometimes they drop:
"I don't do well with stress." In a job where everything is stress and urgency.
So yeah, the kitchen–dining room relationship today isn't always easy.
Because they don't understand the products or us.
And us? We don't understand them or the customers.
Still...
There are the others.

The Idealists
Irreducible believers. And most of them are old-timers. But I've heard and seen a new breed rising amongst the new generation. Whether Americans or Europeans, thank God they still exist.
They say hello with a firm handshake, holding straight as oyster knives
They know the job, their menu, and their grape varieties. They know the difference between doneness levels, seasons, and allergies (the real ones). They can sell a dish because they tasted it. Talk about a product because they respect it.
And above all, they master the clientele with its tantrums and whims.
From twenty meters away, they can tell if one table is about to walk out, if another wants dessert

but won't admit it, and if a third expects the chef to come say hello.
They run their section like directors.
They feel the mood, anticipate drama, and spot the couple about to split up. The table that's going to explode, or the customer who'll send back a wine because it "stings the nose."
They manage a dining room like they're conducting an orchestra—and they understand that serving isn't just bringing a plate.
It's creating an experience.
They take it all.
With a smile.
With swagger.
With class.
They're the ones who keep restaurants running and keep the whole thing standing.

And in the kitchen, we love them.
We always have a little plate ready for them at the end of service when they tell us they're starving.
We respect them because they understand our dishes and because they respect our work.
They're partners. Accomplices. Soldiers in a different regiment but in the same army.
And behind the stoves, we look at them the way we look at the last orangutans or the last record store clerks: with tenderness, admiration... and a little fear for the future.
Because those waiters are worth gold—and they're disappearing too.
They're not valued anymore.
Not respected enough.

And they’re hard to replace.
What the kids coming into hospitality don't understand is that they're the link between the dining room and the kitchen.
A simultaneous translation of kitchen craft for customers. Like a bridge.
And today that bridge is cracked. Nothing has collapsed yet, but it’s shaking.

But as if that weren’t enough—there are the customers.
These tightrope walkers are lost between two worlds: the old one and the new one.
One foot in a short rib drowning in sauce, the other in quinoa.
They want to eat healthy, but they cry the second they smell bone marrow.
They order steamed fish and a salad... then end up stealing bites of their neighbor’s ribeye béarnaise.
They swear they don’t eat meat anymore... except when there’s a duck breast on the special board.
Sometimes adorable. Unbearable other times.
They live in a shaky, unstable balance. Like kids who grew up with Saturday night meals but now feel forced to order a tofu-avocado poke bowl with sesame sauce.
Hybrid beings.
torn between what they think they should eat and what they actually like to eat. They are split by appearances so they don’t look like a boomer.

Stuck between the photo and the sauce, between the image and taste, between the era and their memory.
They eat weird stuff Monday through Friday—nuggets, burritos, tacos, burgers, and pizza. Nothing over three syllables, and anything you can order in three clicks.
And then one night, out of nowhere, it hits them like childhood grief:
"I could really go for a... lamb shank."

And still...
When they order duck confit, when they mop up sauce with bread, I watch them close their eyes. As if someone lights a candle in their memory. Their eyes shine, and they become simple again. They vaguely remember that eating might be something other than an Instagram story.
You see them come back to themselves, like they're walking through Paris streets to the sound of an accordion, and the smell of garlic comes up through their left nostril.
It almost looks like a ghost is stroking their cheek, whispering:
— Go on. You can finish the potatoes. No one will judge you. (Well... except their personal trainer.)
And on those nights, I love them.
Because in those seconds—two seconds, no more—within that suspended moment, there's a reminiscence. A spark of the good old days.
And I tell myself maybe it's not completely screwed.
Not yet.

Not entirely.

But after that minute of grace?
Bam.
They relapse.
They fall back in.
They pull out their phone and ask if the vol-au-vent or the onion soup exists "gluten-free."
If the coq au vin comes "keto," or if the béchamel is lactose-free.
If we can do the fries in an air fryer, "like at home."
That's today's customers: tired modernists, ashamed nostalgics. Old hearts in bodies counting calories. Souls stuck in a world that wants to sanitize everything. They act modern, but their taste buds still belong to the last century.
So we, in the kitchen, laugh. We sigh.
And we keep serving.

If anything I wrote doesn't seem weird to you, it means I'm getting too old for this shit.
For the others, well, imagine Steve McQueen and Frank Sinatra walking into a restaurant and asking if the meatballs are plant-based meat.
Or if the bread pudding is gluten-free and lactose-free.
Since they aren't, they stand up, annoyed, slide their vape back into their pocket, and leave.
Outside, they hop on their electric scooters and ride to the closest juice bar to order a smoothie.

You get the scene.

Not much more to add, right?
Alright, that's a wrap.

Frankenstein

Yes, I admit I have a soft spot for the ancient
world; it was not better or worse, but it was more
compatible with me.
You went to a restaurant.
You ordered.
A plate landed.
You picked up a fork.
You ate.
You left satisfied or disappointed.
It wasn't complicated.

But things have changed.
We Frankensteined the client.
At the beginning of the experience, it sounded
generous, democratic, and modern to make a king
out of him.
We thought we could groom and mold this
creature. But we created a monster. He escaped
the laboratory and set himself free. And we have
lost total control over it.
Now he haunts the dining rooms;
He howls reviews in the dark.
Now he's always right.
And chefs and restaurant owners are responsible.
We made a mistake, and now it's our curse.
In the process, we have turned the restaurant into
administrative offices.
We have let fear and doubt enter into the kitchen,
and doubt followed in the dining room.
Substitution became mechanical.

Automatic.
Pavlovian.
We allowed a system where customers can order a dish with twenty-four lines of modifications.
No garlic.
Sauce on the side.
No butter.
No salt.
Half rare, half well done, grilled but finished in a pan.
What the hell!
Everything is replaced and adjusted until nothing tastes like anything, and the orders look like an appeals court.
The customer doesn't order; he pleads his case.
He doesn't take pleasure; he negotiates.
He doesn't finish your plate; he apologizes.
And he goes home on parole, assigned to house arrest with a doggy bag.

Listen, be realistic. Dishes aren't infinitely customizable. The freedom to undo and redo at will pushed cooks to stop deciding.
Limits create trust, and frames give meaning. The problem is, when everyone wants to be right, everyone ends up wrong.
Choice was supposed to save us; it paralyzed us.
So the menu stops guiding.
And when the plate hits the table, nobody eats right away. It starts with an audit.
You look, analyze, and check if this moral choice will match the person you're trying to be this

week. And if it doesn't, your plate will judge you with every bite.
The worst part?
It works.
Just enough to ruin the dish, not enough for anyone to admit it.
And somewhere along the way, Flavor became suspicious.
Sauce became dangerous because fat is visible.
Butter became ideological.
Joy became optional.
But sugar? Noooooo. Sugar doesn't scare anybody. Sugar is our friend.
Strangely, there's no one complaining there.
Funny.
So in the end, the pleasure is on hold, pending the guest's approval.

We offered multiple-choice menus that you can read like insurance policies.
Don't worry, we put garnishes on the side to anticipate the potential damages to your aura.
Now, we provide you the ingredients, and you are as free as a bird to do whatever you want with them.
But you didn't count on the fact that the responsibility slid onto your shoulders. And instead of sitting down and enjoying your meal, you're under pressure now.
You have to work on your lunch as well.
Build your bowl.
Select your protein.
Choose the veggies

Pick your dressing.
Hurry the fuck up; there's a line behind you.
Once you've finished eating, you get this little gray sad angel tapping your shoulder, whispering:
— You didn't take risks. You made the right choice. A safe choice.
But "safe" is the exact opposite of memorable.
And when food gets infected with this nonsense, everyone bleeds.
The cooks.
The servers.
The customers.
This isn't nostalgia or anger; it's lucidity. The kind that settles in your bones when a system keeps moving but stops making sense.
Nowadays, I am tempted to print a note at the bottom of the menu:
"If you're disappointed, it's partly your fault too.
The longer and more modified the order is,
The smaller the pleasure gets."
We know better than anyone that when texture disappears, balance collapses, and everything turns soft. Harmless.
But go on; don't be scared. You can swallow it now without thinking or feeling, because we've removed fear and guilt, and we slapped blandness on the menus like a substitute seasoning.

There is one thing we haven't talked about.
It is the aftermath...the trauma.
Behind my burners, every service, I witness quiet tragedies and endless pain.

Every night I see a vegetable cry because it just wanted to be cooked in butter. But instead, it ended up steamed, to expiate your sins and his at the same time.

I hear everywhere that everyone wants to eat or cook “authentic" food, but nobody wants to deal with the consequences.
Authenticity has a smell.
It stains.
It leaves marks on the tablecloth, on chef coats...
and sometimes even on your conscience.
You can’t sanitize it.
When food becomes a speech, eating becomes anxiety.
When pleasure has to justify itself, something essential disappears.
But it doesn’t leave quietly.
It leaves screaming because real cuisine doesn’t whisper.
It talks loudly, often with its mouth full.
And it screams that flavor and taste decided to fight back.
Pots and pans have joined the resistance.
It’s about time.
Will you?

Sign of the times

When I was a kid, I was taught to eat everything.
My grandmother used to say, “How can you say you don’t like it if you haven’t tasted it?”
So I tried pretty much everything she put in front of me.
I loved calf’s liver, kidneys, snails, sweetbreads, pig’s ears, or pig’s feet. Chard, salsify, rutabaga, and watercress.
And even today, if any of those dishes are on the menu, I order them without looking at the rest.
Although brains and tripe—that wasn’t my thing, but I knew why: I tasted it.
Regarding cheeses, the rule was simple: the more it smelled, the more it ran in shame.
The happier I was.
And like every kid, I had my childhood ammo:
Kiri cheese, cookies, yogurt, and candies.

Molière said we should eat to live; well, I believe in the exact opposite; I live to eat.
Food is my memory, my thread, my engine.
Without it, I shut down.
And despite the years, my tastes haven’t changed that much:
I still love elbow pasta with ham, sausages, and mashed potatoes; Laughing Cow cheese; a baguette with butter and chocolate powder; and petit-suisses.
I am a hopeless glutton.

And I have to thank my grandparents. They didn't just pass down tastes and flavors. They passed down respect for culinary traditions and gave me an identity through it, a way of being in the world.

Today, I have the awkward feeling that it's become the opposite.
Very early on, parents teach their kids that eating should be practical, fast, and predictable.
Just take a look at a lunchbox; everything is compartmentalized, sealed, and secured.
Nothing leaks, nothing overflows, and nothing surprises. It's gentle, inclusive, and reassuring.
They get exactly what they know or who they want.
We avoid what they dislike.
We don't insist on what they've never tasted.
We no longer help children discover anything else.
So at the cafeteria, on the bus, in the car, and between activities—food fits in the hand, survives the backpack, and can be eaten without upsetting anyone.
The problem is, when those kids grow up, they become coherent adults.
And they eat the way they were trained to.
Without a table.
Without a pause.
Without waiting.
Without memory.
It's not their fault—they're continuing the pattern.

I see it with my own kids.

Do you think the children of a chef are different?
Yeah, right. Dream on.
Despite my attempts to teach them how to cook, they are not into it.
I heard some of the hits from their playlist "Too long," "too complicated," "a waste of time."
The funny thing is, I see them every day, and sometimes I feel like an anthropologist observing a new species, analyzing their feeding habits
It's quite revealing.
When they're hungry, they open the fridge, and they just stand there, like zombies. Staring at God knows what for ages.
And that drives me crazy. So I ask them what they want to eat, and I always get the same answer.
—"Dunnow."
After being shocked by witnessing so much energy and enthusiasm in one individual, I reflect on it, and I get it.
There's no real hunger, no anticipated pleasure, and no desire.
When I look inside the fridge, all I see is the white light illuminating clean, silent, efficient packaging. Everything is ready. Neutral. Pre-chewed, pre-cut, pre-sliced, and pre-cooked by the system. I feel like I'm standing in front of the takeout app.
Eventually, before all hope is gone, they grab something. But they don't pick ingredients to cook a dish. They grab something to fill up.
To silence hunger by pure reflex.
And then they eat without sitting down.
Without a plate.

Without cutlery.
With one hand.
Because that's the way their world keeps spinning.
On the other hand, they can channel surf while the TV talks to itself. Or grab their phone buzzing on the counter, alerting them that social media is calling.
Once they're done, they are calmer; they have something in their stomach, but they're neither full nor satisfied.
And just like that, with a magical plastic trick, the meal disappears exactly as it arrived.
It inspires nothing. Suggests nothing.
It only answers a logistical problem—not an emotional one.
That's when I realize what we've forgotten. What we've lost.
The desire and the joy to stop for a while to eat.

And I see it in restaurants as well.
The meal is no longer a moment—it's a socialized interval.
Being at the table was an assumed pause; now it feels like a glitch. Sitting at it for too long feels suspicious; taking your time looks like an anomaly.
And if you stare at your plate more than a few seconds after photographing it, it already feels like overthinking, excessive.
Food must be fast. Simple. Predictable.
And above all—reassuring.
So people order what they know.

The unknown now feels like a risk.
And risk feels irresponsible.
More and more, guests flinch at anything unfamiliar. Because doubt is seen as a waste of time.
And if they don't like it, the discomfort feels like a personal failure—the regret of not having chosen something else.
A dish used to surprise you.
Now it confirms you.
So taste is no longer an adventure.
It's an insurance policy.
We end up eating the way we think or behave in society:
Logically, with ratios, with fear in our gut.
Inevitably, what follows is an avalanche of diets and "healthy" foods.
Calories in, calories out. Protein ratios. Fat tracking. Controlled balance.
Zero assumed pleasure. Maximum surveillance.
Food has become social fuel—a wellness objective.
We eat to perform, and the more we do, the worse we eat.
The worse we eat, the more we feel guilty.
The more guilty we feel, the more we seek redemption.
And since pleasure no longer sells—but guilt, fault, and forgiveness do—
The system adapts the vocabulary to soothe consciences. When pressure becomes too much, when discipline wears you down, excess is authorized.

But it's a controlled fall. Programmed. Organized. Brutal. Without nuance.
After all that effort and deprivation, you've earned your reward. Your guilty pleasure.
Translation:
Salad at lunch. Burger at night.
Indulge on the weekend. Existential crisis on Monday.
Binge at Christmas and New Year's. Detox in January.
Honestly, I don't have your balance.
I am impressed by those acrobats of permanent tightrope walking.

But the most ironic part?
We call this freedom of choice.
Yes—a choice between two carefully packaged regrets: morality or self-righteousness.
This isn't an individual failure; it's a collective success.
A perfectly oiled system that makes us live in a world that worships performance and mistrusts pleasure. So we're sold functional, marketed food —presented as benevolent.
From what I see, the result is bleak:
souls without cravings, stomachs never satisfied.

The mistake would be to think this is about taste or ignorance; it's deeper than that.
Nowadays we live in an era that has become sanitized, prudent, and afraid.
Anything that feels good is suspicious.

Ecstasy must be justified, framed, and reprimanded.
We no longer eat something because it's good.
We eat it because it's acceptable. Authorized.
Compatible with the image we want to project.
"Healthy" isn't a cuisine—it's a confession.
A way to stay in line, fit the mold.
You know what I think of that fucking mold.
Don't bullshit me—who chooses a salad because it's tempting?
I am 53, and I've never woken up and thought,
"You know what? Today I crave a salad."
You?
Yeah, right, that's what I thought.
You eat it to redeem yourself.
To show you've understood the system.
To prove you are on the right side.
Prove to whom?
The right side of what?
Which line?
Which camp?

We no longer eat for our bodies—we eat for our psychosomatic résumé.
And that virtue has to be visible. Posted. Shared.
In this context, the more I think about it, junk food isn't an aberration.
It's a brilliant idea.
It's become a pressure valve, a decompression chamber.
It lets you crack without a second thought.
Without feeling ashamed.
Without having to justify yourself.

That's the order of things.
La Rochefoucauld said it better than I could:
"Hypocrisy is the homage vice pays to virtue."
So we eat like we work; it's almost Orwellian.
Same logic. Same rhythm. Same gentle madness.
You're not asked to love.
You're asked to endure the day. The pace. The job.
Hold your tongue.
Maintain appearances.
Obey.

In this new world, food is no longer there to bring people together.
It's there to calm—and to send a message.
To calm the fear of being late, of falling behind.
The fear of becoming useless.
We eat to avoid feeling the emptiness that threatens as soon as everything stops.
Silence and stillness have become unbearable. So you always chew—or do something:
a snack, an idea, a goal, a deadline, a post, a reel.
Anything—as long as it keeps you from thinking.
We no longer eat against hunger but against boredom.

To me,
This world doesn't lack food; it lacks pauses.
It doesn't lack spirit; it lacks rebellion.
It doesn't lack recipes; it lacks common sense.
It doesn't lack time; it lacks the will to take it.

I know, in France, we sometimes eat too much.
Meals can be excessive.

Loud, long, messy, and boozy.
But they are embodied.
Now we eat "right." Optimized. Labeled.
Tribalized.
Between orgasmic excess and sanitized optimization, I've chosen my side.
I prefer a plate that overflows to a plate that apologizes.
I prefer a meal that lasts to boredom that never ends.

Another Story

By a happy coincidence, I'm starting to write this chapter on December 30th—and like in any self-respecting restaurant, it's inventory time.
So let's take stock.

I am still behind a stove in Miami, which, statistically speaking, because of my age and being French, already makes me a walking miracle. It makes me feel like an endangered species, but not because of climate change or arthritis.
Don't worry, I am not the protected kind, and thank God, not the Instagrammable one either.
I am more of the bad seed kind, the kind that smells like butter, garlic, and bad decisions made after midnight.
And with all the nasty I've written, all those words spread on these pages like Nutella on crispy toast with a slice of jalapeño, I know I won't end up as the poster child with the label "employee of the month" with the awkward smile.
But I'm not the only one.
I'm not alone.
There are a few of us still standing. Scattered, bruised, but stubborn enough to remain in the kitchen, carrying the weight of being irrelevant.
And lately, it's starting to get on my nerves.

Because I come from a time when you learned by burning your fingers, not by watching a YouTube

tutorial. From a time when cooks learned by fucking up, by burning their fingers.
I'm from the generation that learned how to chop an onion before learning English and who discovered life in walk-ins that smelled like low tide and despair.
Who trained in kitchens without AC, without therapists, without QR codes, or without an HR department on speed dial.
Where there was only one rule:
Just one rule:
Move your ass and don't screw this up.
A world where you tasted everything you didn't understand and weren't afraid of cream.
Where you knew how to choose a melon by smelling its ass.
When butter wasn't political and fat wasn't sociological, that was just what gave flavor.
And if someone asked for cornstarch to thicken a sauce, you would be gently escorted out of the premises. Today? They'd get promoted.
And last but not least, when bread was just... well... bread.

Today, I look around and tell myself I'm a dinosaur in a chef's jacket.
A mammoth in an apron, because I'm on the margins now. Pushed aside.
I've become toxic.
Too French for some. Too senior for others.
Too expensive, too blunt, too loud, too authoritarian—and my favorite—too qualified.
I've heard the full menu of "too" in interviews

these past couple of years. One of these days, I expect someone to tell me I'm too alive.
Yes, I am still breathing, still moving, but clearly not part of the next parade.
Kids are cheaper and more obedient. They don't argue. They don't question. They don't pick a fight.
Me?
I still argue with ingredients, with recipes, and with people, and I've watched more techniques die than colleagues.
Hand-whisked béarnaise (the real one, not the Thermomix one).
Brown stocks reduced for eight hours and sauces that coat the spoon.
Cooking by instinct—with your eyes and your touch—knowing when a meat is ready by touching it, not with a probe thermometer or a laminated chart.
I'm not bitter—and I never have been—but I am lucid.
It's getting tricky trying to manage hypersensitive servers, cooks with shaky hands, and social media aspirations.
Where one-half of customers are tantrum-throwing kings who know their calorie intake better than seasonal vegetables.
Granted, in Miami there are no seasons—but that's not the point.
And the other half is scared of butter and starts wobbling the second the word "gluten" comes up.

In the end, everyone wants pleasure—as long as it's approved by their app, their trainer, and their conscience.

The world changed; I did as well, but at least not enough, and that's the problem.
Because guys like me don't bend well. We're not flexible.
In this hush-hush, inclusive age, we don't whisper. We don't go quietly.
We don't plate "concepts."
We don't cook fear.
So we've become inconvenient.
Too loud.
Too blunt.
Too greasy.
Too honest.
Basically: unmanageable.
You know what? We fought specifically not to fit into the mold. We didn't need to try; we didn't want to.
We adapted just enough to survive, because we didn't want to lose our souls and maybe what we are... or were.
I'm not sure anymore.
And somehow, that became a flaw.

But here's what I've understood.
I'm no longer built to follow modernity—I'm here to resist, to fight in the name of an ideal.
Not for comfort.
Not for peace.

Definitely not for longevity or mental balance (too late for this one).
But fight for my professional survival. Battling cliches about my age and defending my right to keep working in a kitchen
For the pride of saying, "I am in my kitchen, cooking, with my guys, and we never let it go."
Like an old bastard standing in the middle of the walkway, refusing to drop his whip as long as there's a kid left to teach how to mount a beurre blanc at the ass-end of a saucepan.
Sometimes whispering for the attentive and the passionate, sometimes yelling it for the least reluctant one.
To pass on the tradition of effort and comfort.
And also to bear witness.
To tell what was—and what no longer is.
Sharing and helping kids to respect the trade and making them understand talent isn't enough.
It's never enough.
A dish takes work, sweat, and commitment.
It has to be earned.
Finally, to transmit two or three truths that even nutrition coaches won't manage to kill.

I've aged, I know. I complain more than I roar.
Which is probably a sign of senility, or maybe wisdom. Or both.
Old beasts don't sprint anymore; they save strength. Read the terrain.
And when they strike... it's clean. Precise.
So I'm going to sit down for a bit and enjoy this moment of calm.

Let things simmer before going on a charge again and picking the next fight.
Even though I know one day this kitchen will go on without me. That's the rule, and it's fine.
It'll keep going, for sure.
It'll change, probably.
It'll purify itself. More than that? Fuck, I don't see how.
Maybe it'll come back to the essentials—I hope so.

But beware, because this is also a warning.
My time isn't over. And even if it's counted, I'm going to savor every second of it.
Though I am a worn, second-hand transmission belt, I still do the job, and faster and better than the new kids.
So, I'm going to hang around for a while longer.
Standing.
Cooking.
Writing.
Being mildly unbearable and annoying.
I'll stay in kitchens as long as I can.
As long as I love it.
As long as I have the strength—and the pleasure.
And I'll keep writing too.
Dropping truths that aren't always pleasant to hear.
Being the itch that won't go away.
Pissing people off. Cooking.
Because I still have enough in my belly to be useful.

Just not in this world.

Yes, the time is coming to migrate back to where I come from.
where I can find my landmarks.
To a quieter universe that still exists in certain alleys, certain villages, and old-school joints where butter doesn't need an excuse and taste doesn't ask permission.
Where kitchens are still loud, imperfect, and alive.
Where exactly? I don't know yet.
I'll tell you when I've found it.

In the meantime I will think about what I leave behind:
Very loud services and a lot of inappropriate laughter.
Memories, arguments, and brothers and sisters in arms.
Dishes, burns, cuts.
Gestures you don't learn on a phone.
And maybe—just maybe—one or two apprentices who understood that before plating, you taste.
I won't leave with regrets or bitterness.
I never have.
And when I leave, I won't be sad.
I'll leave full.
Full of memories. Full of scars. Full of gratitude—
That magical sauce you don't reduce; you just earn.
And happy.
Because I lived off my passion, and I gave everything I could—everything I had.
And I found a kind of inner peace in it, like when you look at a finished plate before saying,

"Service."
Now I'm preparing to step back—not from life, not from menus—but from this culinary madness that moves too fast to make any sense.
I have deserved it.

The joke has gone on long enough.
It doesn't make me laugh anymore.
I don't have the patience for this bullshit.
So I'm going to let this new generation of cooks run toward God-knows-what.
Guest, do your tofu and salt-free quinoa thing.
Whatever works for you—there must be something for everyone.
Me? I'm going to keep moving and cooking, but at my pace.
Slower, but surer.
And Frenchier by the minute. I own it.
And when I arrive, I'll push open the door of some dive, step behind the stoves, and send out dishes that pay tribute to the good old days.

That's it. I'm done.

Now, if you'll excuse me—reservations are full.
The restaurant is packed, and I've got a herd of starving trolls ready to tear my menu apart with modifications, sauces on the side, and other modern miracles.
If I'm lucky, one of them will ask for a burger cut in half—half rare, half well done.
And if it's really my night, another will ask me to slice his steak.

Funny thing is, a server swore to me they put knives on the tables.
I'm relieved—chopsticks aren't very practical for meat.

Alright. My team is ready, and I hear the printer is starting to get funky
And if one of you happens to be in the dining room tonight,
Bon appétit.
See you on the other side of the window.
Stay hungry, my friends.

Epilogue

This book is for them.
The simple people.
The ones who work, who don't complain, who get up early, and who don't cheat.
The ones who don't "watch what they eat" because they still know what they're eating.
Hopeless romantics who still have taste, heart, and dirt under their nails. And who still knows what it means to wait for something to simmer?

For the grandmas at the grocery store who choose their yogurt carefully.
Not too sweet. Not too sad.
The couples who argue in aisle seven in the supermarket then end up in aisle twelve hand in hand in front of the deli counter, like in front of an altar.
Because a good "dry sausage" fixes everything.
For the mothers who cook a shepherd's pie to bring people together, a mashed potato to calm things down.
A gratin to soothe.
A stew so we don't forget where we come from.

For the loyal nostalgics who still go to their butcher, their cheesemonger, their produce guy, Not out of snobbery—out of faith. Because they like talking about the weather and the taste of tomatoes.
Like a form of prayer.

For the kids who steal radishes from the basket while the parents talk at the market.
And the teenagers biting into a still-warm croissant outside the bakery before school.

For the farmers, the growers, the breeders, and the ones who love their animals, who know their cows by name and talk to their bees.
Who watch their lettuces grow the way others watch their kids grow up, living by the rhythm of the seasons, not by stories.

This book is for those who are still hungry. Not hungry for money, abs, fame, or likes.
But for warm bread, sauce that coats the spoon, and pleasure that sticks to your soul.
For those who know that happiness, sometimes, is just a slice of pâté, a baguette, and a glass of red at the right temperature.

I don't like cookbooks. I like books about sensations and thrills.
About memories.
About life.
The kind that tells stories about the morning coffee and a baguette.
A daily special is on the counter.
A cheese plate and a bottle of burgundy.
A plate of charcuterie and a bottle of Fleurie.
Long story short, scenes of food and meals that smell like roasted meat and friendship.

Conversations that are useless—and therefore essential—celebrating stupidity, rain on cobblestones, and time passing.

See this book as an ode to everything you eat that comforts, satisfies, and makes life better.
A tribute to all those who prefer simple over perfect.
To the Sunday vendors up before dawn.
To brasseries that open early and bistros that close late.
To café owners smiling behind zinc counters.

Here, there's no diet and no promise of longevity.
No sacred quinoa and no magic spirulina.
No air fryers and no freeze-dried bullshit.
Here we chop, we flambé, we reduce, and we taste with our fingers.
We lick the spoon like kids.
It's a kiss that tastes like salted butter.
Like a slap in the face to blandness.
A middle finger to lukewarm food, tasteless plates, and sad dishes with no soul that smell like nothing.
A slap in the face To the cult of emptiness, leveling down, and mediocrity.
A tribute to those who still cook, drink, bicker, and laugh at all this mess.
To the American middle class doing the best it can, fighting in a harsh, unforgiving society.
Hanging on no matter what.
To working-class France—the one that hustles and that has always had more heart than money.

And above all, a thank you to the people who work in restaurants.
Those who walk the dining rooms and serve you.
Those in the kitchen who make daily specials to repair the world.
To all of you who wreck your health, your backs, your nerves, and your voices to offer a brief enchanted pause.
A ray of sunshine in lives that are sometimes too heavy and too dark.
A bit of softness in a brutal world.
To those who still believe in it, who always will.
And who will never give up.

To America, thank you for welcoming me and treating me like one of yours.
To Americans, thank you for letting me cook for you, for the friends and coworkers who became family.
And finally... to France, my country.
the one that made me.
The one I never forgot, even eight thousand kilometers away.
I love you.

To end on a light note, I'll say that food is our shared story.
Our culture.
Our heritage.
Our common good.
I wanted to write a book about the loss of a bond —the loss of eating together.

Because when we no longer sit at the table, we no longer talk.
there. I've done my duty as a citizen.

A republic isn't built only in parliament, congress, or the senate—but at the counter, at the table, and in the kitchen.
And this book is the constitution of mine.
Fine dining is the aristocracy.
The brasserie is the bourgeoisie.
The bistro is the people.
And the café is the public square.
It is ruled for the people and by the people.
Under three fundamental principles.
Not Liberté,
Not Égalité,
Not Fraternité,
But
Food,
Bullshit...
And ...other complications.
And you're all invited.

Postscriptum

I wrote two books because one wasn't enough.
One comes from anger and rebellion—forged in roaring flames.
The other comes from perspective and the understanding of our differences
It was built on embers.
You can read them in order, out of order, or read only one.
There's no rule.
I won't tell you which one to start with.
Or how to understand them.
And even less how to understand me.

I don't write to convince.
And I don't write to exist.
I write to tell stories in the hope that it might be useful to someone.
An apprentice.
A future chef.
A server.
An old-timer who recognizes himself.
A rookie who doesn't know where he's going.
Someone lost, like I once was.
Or a survivor still standing, like I am now.

Both are written.
Published.
They're here, in front of you.
Do whatever you want with them.

The rest belongs to you—and no longer concerns me anymore.

Now I'm going back to my kitchen.
To my dishes, my ovens, my pans.
And to the people I cook for, expecting nothing in return.
Except maybe offering them a small moment of happiness in this ocean of contradictions and harshness we call our daily grind.
Life goes on, and the service never stops.
So, I'll end with the same words I did in my first book:

The kitchen is closed.
I clean my workstation and put my knives away.
And if you come back tomorrow,
there will still be cooks at the kitchen window
and I'll be there, behind the stove...
So you know where to find me.

www.ingramcontent.com/pod-product-compliance
Lightning Source LLC
LaVergne TN
LVHW090606110826
845146LV00001B/282
* 9 7 9 8 9 9 3 1 0 9 5 7 2 *